THE PORTRAITS, PRINTS AND WRITINGS OF JOHN MILTON

GEORGE CHARLES WILLIAMSON

Published by Left of Brain Books

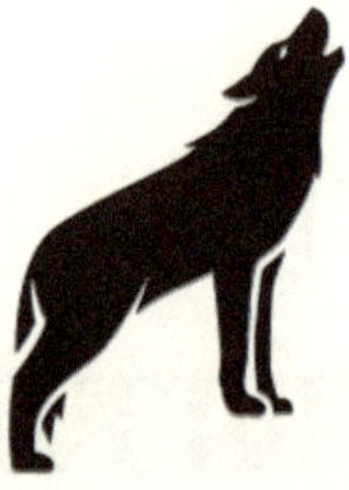

Copyright © 2021 Left of Brain Books

ISBN 978-1-396-32191-7

First Edition

Table of Contents

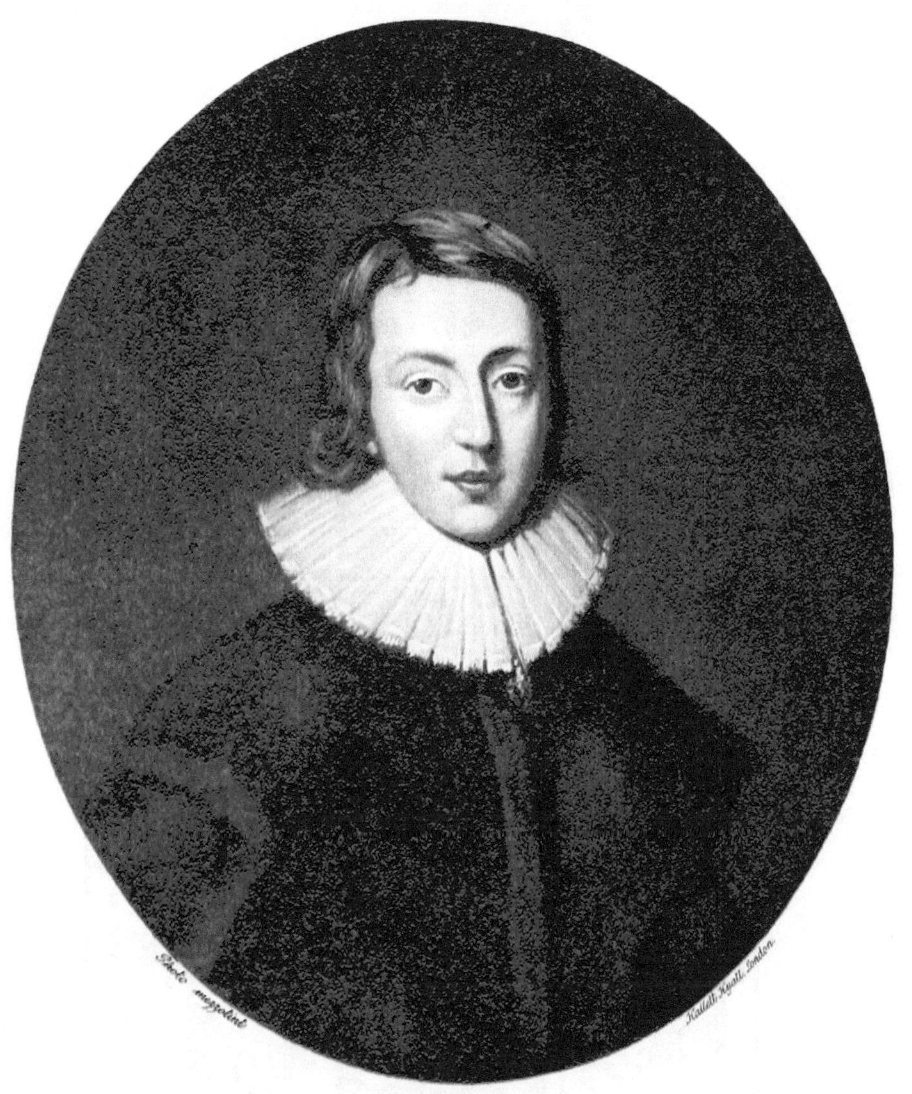

John Milton.
Aged 21.
From the portrait at Nuneham.

Richardus Earle	Lincolniensis filius Augustini, institutus est in literis Grammaticis primo in schola Cantibrigiensi sub auspiciis Mri Bayes, deinde in schola Brantamiensi sub Mro Wilkinson. admissus est pensionarius maior Jan. 11. 1624. anno aetatis 16. sub tutela Mri Chappell. Soluitq pro ingressu	20^d
Robertus Allis.	Sepiensis filius Roberti in agro praedicto, initiatus est in rudimentis Grammaticae primo sub auspiciis Mri Linile scholae Lintoniensis ludimagistri, deinde in schola Audoniensi sub Mro Britten. admissus est Sizator Feb. 3. 1624. sub Mro Knowester Soluitq pro ingressu	5^d
Johannes Milton.	Londinensis filius Johannis institutus fuit in literarum elementis sub Mro Gill Gymnasij Paulini praefecto. admissus est pensionarius minor. Feb. 12. 1624. sub Mro Chappell. Soluitq pro ingressu	10^d

Copy of the entry in the Admission Book, Christ's College.

PREFACE

John Milton, born in Bread Street, London, 9 December 1608, was admitted a pensioner of Christ's College 12 February 1625, according to the modern reckoning—1624, according to the old style in the Admission Book. He resided apparently without a break until he was admitted to the M.A. degree, 3 July 1632. Tradition assigns to him rooms on the first floor of staircase N on the left side of the First Court as you enter by the great gateway; but it is certain that in the seventeenth century each set on the first floor was occupied by a Fellow, at most with his attendant sizar; Milton however was not a sizar. He must have had two or three fellow-students as joint tenants; the College was very full, and there existed only the First Court, a block of buildings, called Rats' Hall, in the middle of the present second Court, and an inn called the Brazen George, adjacent to St Andrew's Church, improperly used to hold undergraduates: the "Fellows' Building" dates from 1642. His life here has been often told—copiously, but with judgment, by Prof. Masson. It is likely that he was not loved by his equals in age, for he was "not ignorant of his own parts," and it is quite conceivable that he gave a grudging obedience to those who were placed over him, the Master, Dean and Head Lecturer; certainly he was on bad terms with his first tutor, William Chappell (afterwards Bishop of Cork) by whom he was transferred to Nathaniel Tovey, but the story of his flogging by Chappell rests (as I have pointed out in my *History of Christ's College*, p. 146) on untrustworthy evidence. Beyond a doubt he was appreciated as he deserved by the Master and Fellows Before he left Cambridge and might well have been elected to a Fellowship, had he been prepared to take Holy Orders (*ib.* 148). But he cast the chance behind him. In his early life that is clearly traceable a resolute ambition, combined with a rare mental balance. He knew his strength, knew what he could do, knew that he would do it. There was a great work before him: he must be thoroughly prepared. So he left Cambridge for Horton, to enter upon a second period of preparatory study in which he was to be his own guide; but that period produced such finished work as *L'Allegro* and *Il Penseroso* (probably written in 1632), *Arcades, Comus* (in 1634), *Lycidas* (1637). His most memorable poems while he was at Christ's are the lines *On the death of a fair infant* (1626), *On the morning of Christ's nativity* (1629), *An epitaph on the Marchioness of Winchester* (1631), *Sonnet on arriving at the age of Twenty-three* (1631). Ample specimens of his exercises both in the College and in the Schools are given by Prof. Masson in his first volume.

Each year we hold our domestic commemoration of all our benefactors and worthies. This year gives to us an opportunity, which we welcome, not only of dwelling upon our connexion with John Milton—"for we were nursed upon the self same hill"—but also of asking others to join us in a commemoration of one whose preeminence among those reared in this College can be questioned in favour of none save perhaps of Charles Darwin. We ask all to enjoy with us the sight of portraits, of books, of other objects which have interest by their relation to Milton. We believe that no collection so large has been previously made; to make it needed special knowledge and unusual zeal and energy, for which we owe a very great debt to Dr. G. C. Williamson and to Mr. Charles Sayle—a debt all the greater that we cannot claim them as members of our body. Dr. Williamson has contributed the following account of Milton portraits, has lent us many of which he is the owner, and has procured us the loan of others: he has also dealt with early editions of the poems: Mr. Sayle has contributed an appendix on editions and on books about Milton to be found at Cambridge. Among those who have been lenders special thanks are due to the Earl of Ellesmere, to Lord Sackville, to Lord Leconfield, to the Right Hon. Lewis Harcourt, to H. Clinton Baker, Esq., to Mrs. Morrison, to J. F. Payne, Esq., M.D. to the Library Syndicate, and to the Master and Fellows of Trinity College; to the University Press, Oxford, to Messrs Sotheran and Co., Pickering and Chatto, and George Bell and Sons.

JOHN PEILE.

CHRIST'S COLLEGE LODGE,
    5 June, 1908.

John Milton was born the 9th of December
1608 die Veneris half an howr after 6 in the
morning
Christofer Milton was born on Friday about
a month before Christmass at 5 in the morning
1615
Edward Phillips was 15 year old August 1645
John Phillips is a year younger about Octob.

My daughter Anne was born July the 29th
on the fast at eevning about half an houre
after six 1646
My daughter Mary was born on Wedensday
Octob. 25th on the fast day in the morning about
6 a clock 1648.
My son John was born on Sunday March the
16th about half an hower past nine at night 1650
My daughter Deborah was born the 2d of May
being Sunday somwhat before 6 of the clock in the
morning 1652.
This my wife hir mother dyed about 3 days after. And my
son about 6 weeks after his mother
Katherin my daughter, by Katherin my second wife, was
borne ye 19th of October, between 5 and 6 in ye morning,
and dyed ye 17th of March following, 6 weeks after hir
mother, who dyed ye 3d of Feb. 1657

Page from John Milton's Bible, in the British Museum, giving the entries made with his own hand relative to the birth of himself and various members of his family.

THE PORTRAITS OF JOHN MILTON.

Collectors of prints have long been troubled by the strange and perplexing variety of portraits, said to represent John Milton, which, from time to time, they have obtained; and more than one writer has endeavoured to set forth clearly some statement respecting these portraits. There was not, however, any scholarly attempt to grapple with the complexity of the subject until 1860, when Mr. John Fitchett Marsh, who had been for many years a collector of the engraved portraits of the poet, prepared an elaborate treatise concerning them, which he read before the Historic Society of Lancashire and Cheshire and published in the *Transactions of the Society*, Vol. XII. He was able, on that occasion, to exhibit to the members of the Society over 150 prints and grouped them out, with considerable judgement, under various headings. To his list, all later collectors owe a very great deal, and it has been accepted as a standard by which the value and extent of other collections may be measured; while the theories set forth by Mr. Marsh have, as a rule, been accepted. He, however, laboured under one special difficulty, as he was not acquainted with either of the original portraits of the poet and his arguments were based, almost exclusively, upon the engravings he himself possessed. In this respect, we have at the present time, one advantage over him, inasmuch as two of the authentic portraits of the poet are available, and of a third there is a perfect copy in existence, which may be taken to represent the original. Mr. Marsh's list of engravings was a considerable advance upon any previous list. Granger referred to 37 portraits, Bromley to 25, Evans to 42, Marsh to 164, and although the latter compiler does not appear to have omitted anything of any special importance, yet we are able to add some to his list and to subjoin information respecting over 180 portraits. It may be well to refer briefly to the various groups of which the collection is composed.

The first relates to those engravings copied from the portrait of Milton at the age of ten, and this special portrait, perhaps the most important of all, has only been traced while these pages were being passed for press[1]. It is the picture referred to by Aubrey in his notes written shortly after Milton's death; "Ao. Dni. 1619. He was ten yeares old, as by his picture and was then a poet: his school master was then a Puritan in Essex, who cut his (i.e. Milton's) hair short." It was one of the pictures which remained in the possession of Milton's widow (his third wife) until her death in 1727, and was enumerated in the inventory of her effects at Nantwich. On June 3rd, 1760, it was purchased by Mr. Thomas Hollis, the republican (1720-1774), to whom we shall have occasion to refer several times. He was an ardent admirer of Milton, a strong patriot, the editor of Toland's *Milton*, 1761, of Algernon Sidney's work, 1772, and a generous benefactor to Harvard, Berne, Zurich and Cambridge, giving to the public institutions in these places, books and portraits relating to the heroes of the Commonwealth, the objects of his admiration. On his decease he left his estate to his friend Thomas Brand who assumed the name and arms of Hollis, and he, in his turn, bequeathed The Hyde and its contents, and a considerable estate, to his friend, the Reverend Dr. Disney (who afterwards wrote a memoir of Thomas Brand Hollis), and in the possession of his descendant, the estate still remains.

The Milton portrait was bought at the sale of the effects of Mr. Charles Stanhope, who had mentioned to Mr. Hollis, two months before, that he had bought it of the executors of Milton's widow, for twenty guineas. Hollis gave thirty-one guineas for it and valued it as the choicest of his possessions. On one occasion when a fire broke out in Mr. Hollis's chambers, this was the only possession he was anxious to save, and his biographer tells us, that after he had slipped his purse into his pocket, he went calmly out into the street, carrying the Milton portrait in his hands. It passed with the rest of his possessions to Dr. Disney and eventually to his grandson, Mr. Edgar Disney. Professor Masson described it as a portrait set in a dark oval, about 27 inches by 20 inches in size including the frame, and having the words "John Milton aetatis suae 10 anno 1618" inscribed on the paint in contemporary characters. Hollis had a careful drawing and etching made of it by Cipriani, and that forms No. 1 in our catalogue of the prints. It may be mentioned here that the Hollis prints, of which there are four, are to be found on both green and white paper,

---

[1] See subsequent note, p. 131, and the *Times* of 3 June, 1908.

those on the former being the most rare; there is also, of one of them, a proof before letters in the author's collection. The picture was attributed to Cornelius Janssen, who is styled on the Hollis print "Johnson," but who receives the more correct spelling of his name, on a further print from the same picture, when it belonged to Mr. Thomas Brand Hollis, who had it engraved by Gardiner for Boydell's sumptuous edition of Milton's works in 3 Vols., royal folio. When the picture was in Mr. Edgar Disney's possession it was photographed, and a charming engraving was made by Edward Radclyffe, which forms the frontispiece to Masson's *Milton*.

The only other youthful portrait of the poet, is one which appeared in the *Gentleman's Magazine* for September 1787, engraved almost in outline. It was accompanied by a letter, dated from Oxford, sending the drawing from which the portrait was engraved, and which the letter states "A friend who lives there has obligingly suffered to be taken from a picture in his possession. It is on wood. At top is Ao. 1623. aet suae 12. In the hands of the figure is a book with Homers Iliads on the leaves. The hair is red. This drawing is very like, only perhaps somewhat older than the picture." There is a good deal of complexity respecting this picture. It certainly closely resembles the one by Janssen and has many resemblances to what we know of Milton's personal appearance, especially in the fact that the colour of his hair was certainly reddish in his early days. The date however cannot be accurate. It is either misprinted in the *Gentleman's Magazine*, which seems likely to be the case; or else there is a mistake with regard to the age of the boy; but the question cannot be readily dismissed, because of the resemblance in features and it seems just possible that there was then in existence, and may be even so now, an almost unknown portrait of Milton as a boy with some claims to authenticity. The drawing was referred to in the same volume on page 892 by a correspondent who pointed out the striking resemblance it bears to the Cipriani print, but this second correspondent started a confusion about the dates, which, by the way, seems to have been rather a feature of the whole controversy; no one engraver or collector taking adequate pains to verify dates and information.

We now come to the second of the two portraits enumerated in the inventory of Mrs. Milton's effects, and here again unfortunately we have to state that the original work is not available for comparison or study. Its disappearance is even more remarkable than the loss of the Hollis-Disney portrait. Aubrey, who wrote in 1681, refers to the picture as follows: "his widowe has his picture drawne (very well and like) when a Cambridge schollar: she has his picture when a Cambridge schollar which ought to be engraven; for the pictures before his books, are not at all like him."

In 1721 Deborah Clarke, Milton's daughter, informed George Vertue that her stepmother, if living, in Cheshire, had two portraits of Milton, one when he was a school boy, to which we have just alluded, and another when he was about twenty. In 1731, four years after Mrs. Milton's death, the picture was in the possession of Mr. Speaker Onslow, and was engraved by Vertue, and as late as 1794 it was stated in the inscription to the engraving in Boydell's *Milton* to be "in the possession of Lord Onslow at Clandon, in Surrey, purchased from the executors of Milton's widow by Arthur Onslow Esq., speaker of the House of Commons, as certified in his own hand writing at the back of the picture." Speaker Onslow was a notable collector of portraits, and amongst all he possessed, valued this one the most highly. He had a great friend, Lord Harcourt, who was keenly anxious to possess the portrait, but he refused to part with it, consenting, however, to have a perfect copy made of it, if Lord Harcourt in his turn, would have a portrait he possessed, of Pope, by Kneller, copied for him. The work was carried out by Benjamin Van der Gucht, Vertue's master, and although the copy he made of the Kneller, has disappeared, that of the Milton, is still in existence, and by the kindness of the Right Honourable Lewis Harcourt, M.P., is shown in this exhibition, having been removed for that purpose from Nuneham (see frontispiece to this book). It is a faithful copy, as Van der Gucht tells us in the long inscription he has placed upon its reverse, *see under Portraits*. The original was sold in 1828 for the sum of £8. 12*s*. 0*d*. to a purchaser named Moore who was declared to be "not a dealer." It is curious to note that the same name, Moore, appears in connection with the next portrait to be mentioned. At the same sale there were many other portraits sold, some of the chief being as follows. Sir Thomas More £4. 16*s*. 0*d*., Thomas Cromwell £4. 15*s*. 0*d*., Sir Walter Raleigh £3. 18*s*. 0*d*., Bacon £4. 18*s*. 0*d*., Spenser £4. 4*s*. 0*d*., Pope £4. 12*s*. 0*d*., Dryden by Kneller £1, Sir I. Newton, oval, £4, Sir Charles Lucas by Dobson £21, Lord Somers in robes as Chancellor, 1695, and Dr. Burnet, 1690, a pair, £5. 10*s*. 0*d*., Dudley, Earl of Leicester £6. 6*s*. 0*d*., Queen Elizabeth £6. 6*s*. 0*d*., Henrietta

Maria £15. 10*s*. 0*d*., William III £10. 10*s*. 0*d*., George I £3. 5*s*. 0*d*., George II £5. 5*s*. 0*d*. An interesting miniature copy of the lost Onslow portrait is exhibited by Mr. Arthur E. Shipley.

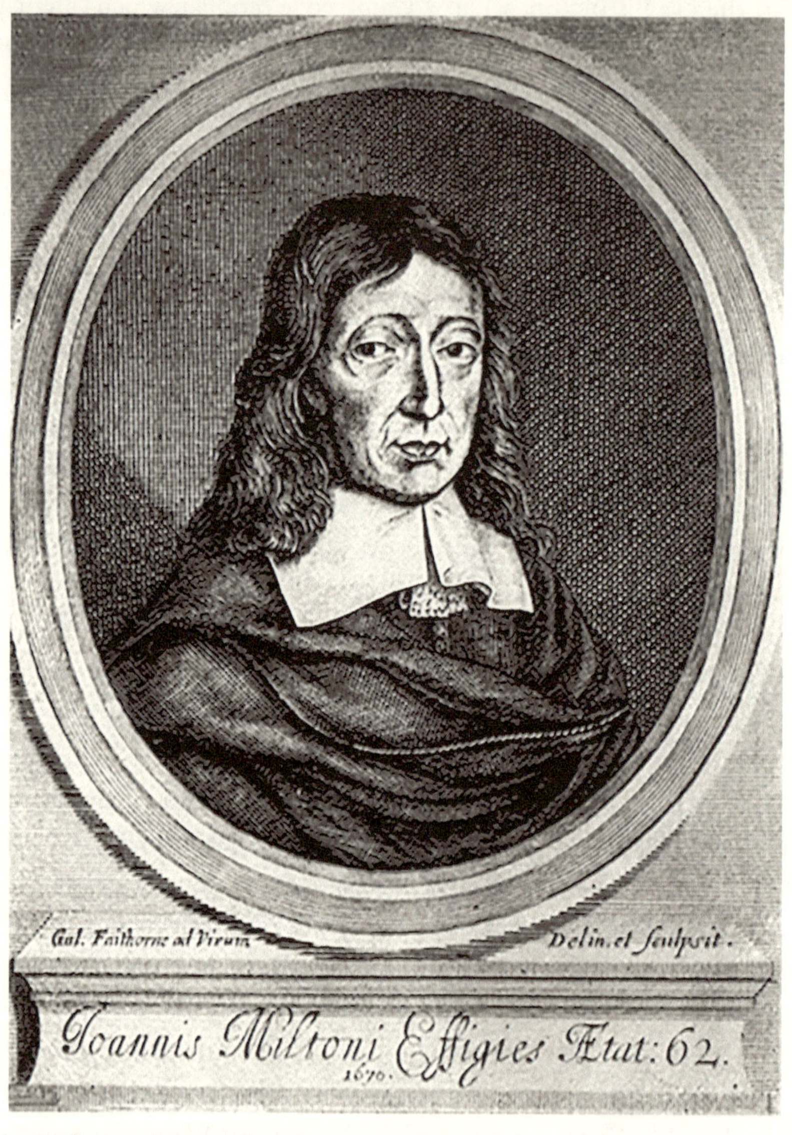

John Milton at the age of 62. Engraving from life by William Faithorne, from Milton's *History of Britain*, 1670. See (24).

Of the Onslow portrait there are many prints. The chief is, of course, the one by Vertue dated 1731, and of it there are two or three varieties, one of extreme rarity. Then there is the Houbraken portrait, executed in Amsterdam in 1741, for which it is believed Mr. Shipley's miniature was the model, as Houbraken was unable to come to England and it does not appear that the original Onslow portrait was ever sent abroad. The engraved copper plate for this Houbraken engraving has recently been acquired by Mr. Shipley, and excellent prints from it have been struck off. There is a late German reproduction of the Onslow portrait and more than one lithograph, and an interesting print which appeared in the *London Magazine* and, altered in size, in the *British Biography*. In 1785 the Onslow portrait was engraved by Goldar for Harrison's edition of *Rapin*; but the two best known engravings from it are, first, the one prepared by Cipriani for Thomas Hollis, having beneath it Milton's sonnet "How soon hath time," etc.; and the other made for Boydell's *Milton* in the time of Mr. Thomas Brand Hollis, and engraved, like the one by Janssen, by W. N. Gardiner in 1794. Proofs before letter are known of each, that of the former being in our possession.

In considering the prints from this exceedingly interesting portrait, we must not overlook one which appeared in Macrone's edition of Milton's works edited by Sir Egerton Brydges, in which Edwards was the engraver. The portrait is clearly the Onslow one, see (19*a*), but by a slip on the part of the engraver, Janssen is declared to have been the original painter, a confusion having been made between this Onslow portrait and the one of Milton at the age of ten. We do not know at all who was the painter of the Onslow portrait and have no means of forming any theory about it, as it is clear that Van der Gucht did not know whose work it was, and we have not now the original picture to refer to.

In 1645, Humphrey Moseley's original edition of Milton's poems was brought out, and William Marshall was employed to produce a portrait as a frontispiece. This is the rare and precious engraving signed W. M., which has beneath it the Greek epigram, composed by the poet, in which he laughs to scorn the fact of its being a likeness of him. There are certain slight resemblances between it and the Onslow picture; they are very slight and in some respects it even more closely resembles the Janssen portrait, but it cannot be accepted in any way as a satisfactory representation of the great poet, and we know in fact, from the epigram "In effigiei ejus sculptorem," how dissatisfied Milton was with the manner in which Marshall had produced the engraving. The generally accepted theory, to which Horace Walpole refers, was that Marshall, who frequently worked for Moseley, drew from life; and Vertue seems to have adopted this theory, but it is hardly possible that it was so; and in the fact that in the next important portrait of Milton, the artist expressly declares that it was drawn from life, there lies an argument against the statement, that Marshall drew the actual portrait from the poet himself. His engraving is evidently to a great extent imaginary and cannot be said to represent the poet at thirty-seven, being in fact much more of the nature of a caricature. As already mentioned, the print of it is rare, and it has not hitherto been easy to obtain a fine impression of the later printing from it which appeared in *Samson Agonistes* in 1848. The plate for this later printing however, which belonged to Evans, has now come into the market and will probably be acquired by Christ's College. There is also a reduced copy, signed by Van der Gucht, which is in Tonson's edition of *Paradise Regained*, 1713, and in which the same Greek inscription, laughing the engraver to scorn, is solemnly rendered by the new engraver, happily, it is to be hoped, ignorant of the condemnation he was unwittingly calling down upon himself. It may, we take it, be granted that there is no original to be looked for in respect to this engraving. It is hardly likely that it would have been kept, even if a preparatory drawing for the engraving was ever made.

If the head of Erato in the W. M. engraving is carefully examined the difference between the original and the later plate will at once be noticed. In the original the head is full of careful modelling, in the later one almost blank. The Van der Gucht reduction omits the four Muses altogether.

When we approach the next portrait we are on surer ground and fortunately the original is still in existence. It is, as Marsh reminds us, the only likeness of the poet taken at a mature age and published with what we may deem his consent during his life time, and it has been the subject of more frequent copies than any other print. The original impression, in which the poet is declared as being sixty-two years old, is dated 1670, and the engraving, which appeared in Milton's *History of Britain*, for that year, bears the name of the artist, William Faithorne, and the express statement that it was both drawn and engraved by him, and from life. The first state of the print bore the date 1670 and this state is of extreme rarity, Louis Fagan declaring in his book on Faithorne, that in the Roupell sale, July 5, 1887, a print of it (Lot 127) fetched £31. This is a price which would be enormously increased if the print were now to come into the market. Of the early history of the original drawing we know very little. It is believed to have been in the possession of the Tonsons, the publishers, and there seems to be some evidence that this is the case, but the confusion between this and the next drawing to be referred to, which certainly was in the possession of the Tonsons, is twice confounded, and although Marsh goes into the matter exceedingly carefully, yet he is not able to disentangle the various statements made by different authors concerning two portraits, one of which certainly belonged to the Tonsons and both of which may have been in their possession. The so-called Faithorne, which represents the poet in a dark dress with white collar, tied with tassels, and long flowing hair, is a bust portrait, painted on canvas, measuring 23 inches by 18 inches. It was exhibited at the South Kensington Museum in 1866, No. 820, and was then in the possession of Mr. Edmund F. Moore. It is pretty clear why he acquired it, inasmuch as his grandmother was Anne, the daughter of Thomas Agar of the Crown Office, London, by Anne Milton, his wife, who was the daughter of John Milton of Bread Street and the sister of John Milton the poet. This Anne Agar married David Moore of Sayes Court, Chertsey, great grandson of Thomas Moore, secretary to Queen Anne Boleyn. Their son was a certain Sir Thomas Moore, who married Elizabeth Blunden, and their son Edmund was the owner of the picture in 1866. No doubt his intimate connection with the Milton family was the reason for his acquiring the portrait, inasmuch as through the failure of descendants in the male line the representation of the Milton family was then, and is still, vested in David Moore's descendants. The present owner of the picture, Sir Robert Henry Hobart, K.C.V.O., C.B., M.P., is the son of Edmund Moore's great granddaughter, and the leading male representative of the Milton family. There is little doubt on comparing the portrait and the print, as to the authenticity of the former, but it should be remarked that in the engraving Faithorne has somewhat accentuated the deep hollows and heavy shadows in the poet's features beyond what is to be seen in the drawing, giving Milton a somewhat more worn expression than he has in the original; the arrangement and shape also of the collar are different. It should be remarked that an absolute comparison is not very easy to make, inasmuch as the engraving is reversed, and further that in Vertue's engravings the features are somewhat softened, a little more closely resembling the Faithorne original, but even more accurately resembling the Bayfordbury picture, to which we next make reference. An illustration of the Hobart picture is given herewith.

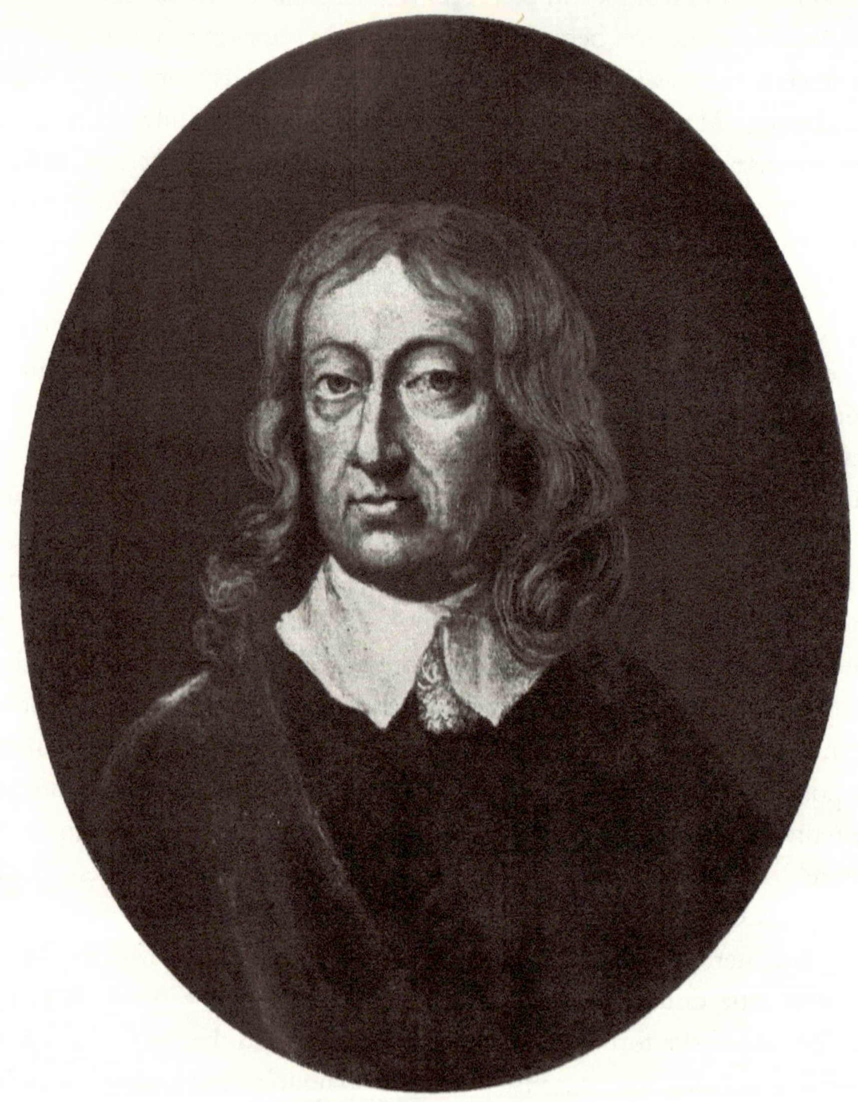

John Milton, by Faithorne. From the original work in the possession of Sir Robert H. Hobart, K.C.V.O., M.P.

When we come to consider the engraving, No. 31 in Marsh's list, we have, entering upon the scene of action, another person, to wit Robert White. This man comes in to make the problem a little more confusing. He was a draftsman and engraver, born 1645, died 1703, and drew very beautifully in pencil on paper or vellum. He was a pupil of David Loggan, whose manner he followed in his pencil portraits; and he engraved a long series of portraits of contemporary characters, mostly from his own drawings, which in the majority of cases were from life. One of the best known of his pencil portraits is that of Bunyan, which is in the British Museum. With regard to the portraits of Milton, his name first appears on the oval portrait published in the fourth edition of *Paradise Lost*, folio, 1688 (see illustration), for which he appears to have been the engraver. The portrait is, however, identical with the Faithorne one, in almost every respect, even down to the buttons on the vest. A little later, however, we find this same man's name appearing as the draftsman on a mezzotint by I. Simon, which is inscribed "R. White ad Vivum delin," and it would therefore appear as though we have to search for a drawing by this artist, which it is quite possible may some day be found. To this mezzotint we refer a little later on.

As regards the Faithorne, the first impression is a fine strong print (see illustration), a later one is not, however, so good. Flatman's compliment to Faithorne has often been quoted and is referred to by Marsh. He said,

> "A 'Faithorne sculpsit' is a charm can save
> From dull oblivion and a gaping grave,"

and, as Marsh points out, the original impression of the Faithorne print is a worthy work of this clever artist, but the later one is not in his best manner, and a third, which is declared as being the original plate reduced, is quite evidently from another plate altogether, which may or may not have been the work of Faithorne.

We now approach the engravings by Vertue, usually grouped together, and so arranged by Marsh, as connected with the Faithorne drawing, but in our opinion these early Vertue prints have a very close resemblance to the Bayfordbury portrait, although at the same time they are derived from the Faithorne one. As regards the Bayfordbury portrait, it originally belonged to Jacob Tonson (1656?-1736), who owned the Kit-Cat Club collection, and it now hangs at Bayfordbury Park, near Hertford, the seat of Mr. H. Clinton Baker, who originally possessed the manuscript of "Paradise Lost" recently sold at Sotheby's. It is not very clear to whom we ought to attribute this drawing. As a rule it is given to Faithorne, and Fagan includes it with the Hobart one in his list of Faithorne's works. It is most probable that this is the case, but it has also been suggested whether it is the work of Richardson, and to this theory an allusion will be made presently. What we want, however, to point out with regard to it, is, that the early Vertue engravings, dated 1720, 1747, and so on, bear in features an exceedingly close resemblance to the Bayfordbury picture, far closer than to the Faithorne drawing, which it may be well to style the Hobart picture. These two pictures are not identical, although they very closely resemble one another. In each the hair is arranged in identical fashion, the collar, tassels, vest and cloak are the same, the lines of the collar following exactly the same curves, and the folds of the gown in the Bayfordbury picture, although not exactly the same, resembling those in the Hobart picture very closely; but the expression is distinctly smoother in the Bayfordbury than in the Hobart picture: and the Vertue engravings more closely resemble it, whereas in the arrangement of the collar with its pendant tassels the Vertue prints resemble neither portrait and are very much closer in appearance to the original Faithorne engraving, being almost identical with it as regards the lines of the collar and the position of the tassels which fall beneath it. We cannot help feeling therefore that, although Vertue's early prints were taken either from Faithorne's engraving or from the drawing from which it was made, yet that Vertue must have had before him the Bayfordbury picture, and, copying all the details of the vest, gown, collar and tassels exactly from Faithorne, took the features much more from the Bayfordbury picture instead of softening down, as Marsh says he did, the somewhat harsh expression of the Faithorne engraving. There are a great many varieties of the Vertue prints, differing in small details, but all showing a common origin, and that origin is revealed in the arrangement of the collar and tassels. In the Hobart and Bayfordbury pictures the collar is a soft, somewhat narrow one, the two points of it spreading apart and revealing the tassels which lie close up to the point of the collar seen on the spectator's right. This characteristic we shall see presently in the Simon mezzotint. In the Faithorne print on the other hand, the collar is broad, square and Genevan in shape, the two points of it coming very close to one another, and the two tassels or lace ends (it is not very clear which) falling below the centre of the collar just by the opening.

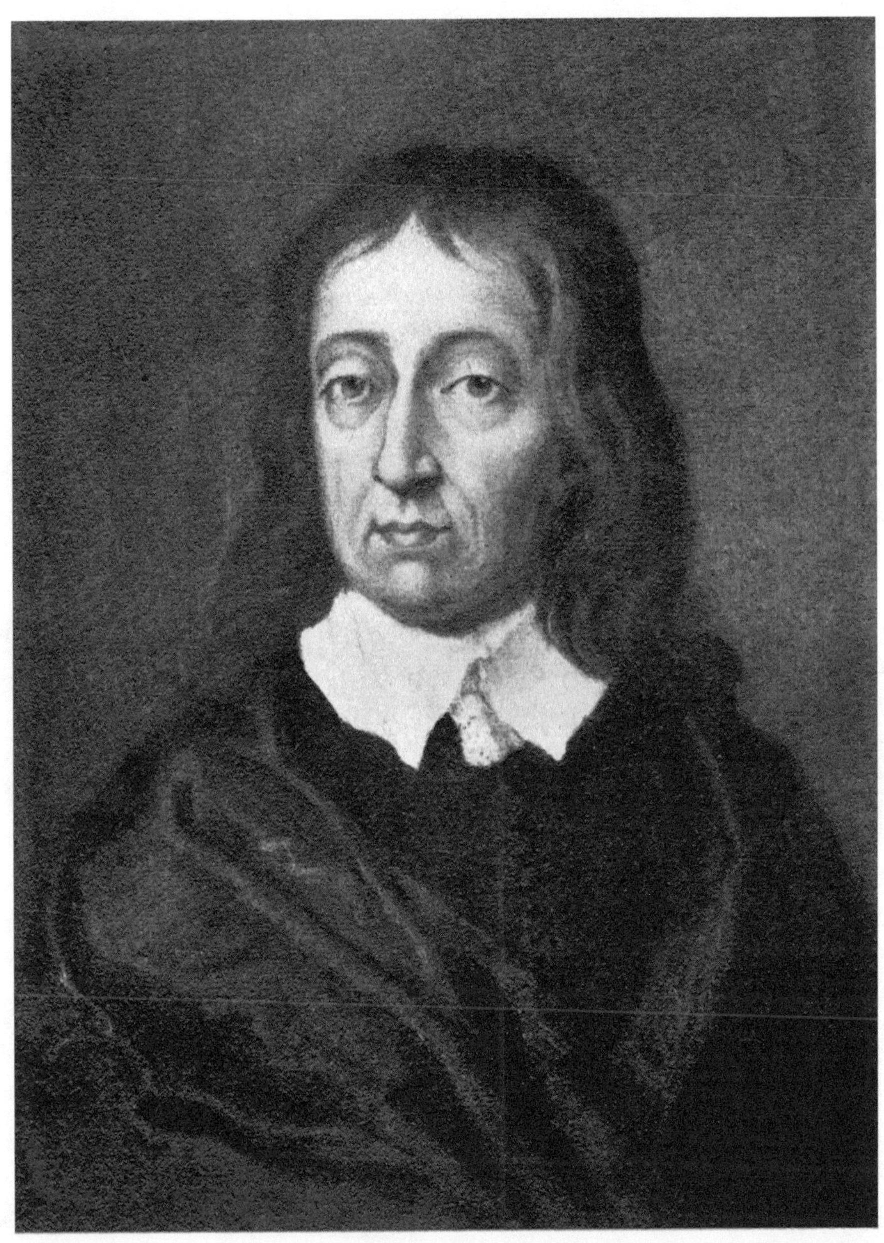

John Milton, from the original portrait known as the Bayfordbury (or Tonson) one
now in the possession of H. Clinton Baker, Esq.

Amongst these prints should be specially noticed one engraved by Kyte in
a set of four poets which appears to have escaped the attention of Mr. Marsh.
One of the most creditable is that published in June 1796 for Richter's edition

of *Paradise Lost*, quarto, 1794, and one of the finest pieces of recent engraving is the oval by H. Robinson published in 1831 in Pickering's Aldine edition. The print by W. C. Edwards, (50), 50*a*, 50*b*, has the same softened expression, which can be seen in (33) and (34), even more accentuated.

The rarest of all is the small mezzotint by Simon, clearly taken from the Faithorne print, but not from either the Hobart or Bayfordbury pictures. Here again the features are softened from their original austerity. The engraving by Cook, 53*a*, and the line engraving by Adlard, 53*c*, on the other hand, were, it should be noticed, taken direct from the Hobart picture and are identical with it in the arrangement of collar, cord and tassels. They are certainly *not* derived from the Faithorne or Vertue print, although they claim to be.

We now come to a group of prints which Marsh arranges as those derived from the Faithorne portrait, and are face to face with a difficulty almost at once. No. (54) one of the Hollis prints, is declared as having been etched by Cipriani at the desire of Thomas Hollis from a portrait in crayons, now in the possession of Messrs Tonson, booksellers in the Strand. It is perfectly certain, however, that the crayon portrait mentioned on this print, is neither the Hobart nor the Bayfordbury picture, although we know that one of these belonged to Tonson and we believe that both of them were once in that gentleman's possession. The arrangement of the collar and tassels absolutely precludes the possibility of this being the case. The print is identical with the Faithorne print, and the folds of the gown, the buttons of the vest, the arrangement of the hair, and the shape of the mouth follow the Faithorne print exactly, and differ in all these respects from the Hobart and Bayfordbury pictures. The etcher has let his own fancy lead him astray with regard to the length of the hair and the position of the eyes, which in Faithorne's engraving are both turned to the spectator's left and in the Cipriani etching face the spectator; but in other respects he has followed Faithorne's print exactly, and therefore if the statement on the print is correct there is yet another authentic portrait to be sought for, the one in crayons done by Faithorne for his engraving, and if that is so it would appear as possible that a third portrait of Milton was in the possession of Messrs Tonson, in addition to the Hobart and Bayfordbury portraits, and that one has never yet been discovered. The whole thing may be a mistake of Cipriani's, or it may point to the existence of a third Faithorne drawing.

Continuing down Marsh's list, we now come to what he calls the White portrait, Simon's rare folio mezzotint, on which there are two states, both included in the author's collection; and in it we have a representation closely resembling the Bayfordbury portrait, and also to a great extent the Hobart portrait. The arrangement of the collar and tassels is identical with both of them, even to the little loops of string, from which the tassels hang, but both the Bayfordbury and Hobart pictures show many more buttons to the vest than appear in Simon's mezzotint, and the folds of the gown which fall from the shoulder are not identical with either of these two known originals. The features, however, can hardly have been taken from anything but the Bayfordbury portrait, and then enters in another theory, because Simon's mezzotint represents the poet with a laurel wreath and that wreath appears in the next group of engravings, called the White-Richardson likeness, and which Richardson declared was taken from an excellent original (crayons) in his possession. Yet at the same time the Simon mezzotint is inscribed "R. White ad Vivum delin." The theory we suggest, to account for the complication, is that the White mezzotint and the Richardson etchings were both taken from the Bayfordbury picture, which may or may not have been the work of Faithorne, and may or may not have been the work of Richardson. Richardson does not actually claim it. He says it is in his collection, but it is spoken of by his contemporaries as being his own work. This statement we are disposed to doubt. That the Bayfordbury picture is the work of Robert White, we do not in the least believe, and have no evidence whatever to connect White with a large portrait such as this one is. It is, however, more likely that White made a fine pencil drawing from the Bayfordbury picture and added to it the laurel wreath, which is of course an addition (and actually so stated, by Richardson in his Explanatory Note, 1674), diminished the number of buttons in the vest, and slightly re-arranged the folds of the gown, and that from his drawing Simon made his mezzotint (which it will be seen, (67a), has been copied in Germany), and Richardson made his etchings, altering again the portrait in certain respects in order to please himself. There must have been the intervention of a drawing because of the presence of the laurel wreath, which later on Richardson omitted, and because the figure is turned round rather more fully to the spectator, revealing the vest in the centre of the portrait, and, in the case of Richardson's etchings, adding two lines on either

17

side of the buttons, and in White's drawing one such line: to show the opening of the vest. Richardson altered the number of leaves in the wreath in two of his etchings, one having nine leaves on the right temple and the other eleven; and in his final work be omitted the wreath altogether, greatly improving the portrait, and added six lines beneath it which are signed "J. R. jun.," and were probably the work of the son, while the father himself, we take it, was responsible for the etching.

These Richardson etchings appeared in 1734, and are alluded to by the artist in *Explanatory Notes and Remarks on Milton's Paradise Lost*. The original plates for them all belonged to Evans, and now to Christ's College. The final portrait (74), which is the best, was issued both in brown and in black ink. In the former it is rare; the Rev. J. W. Cartmell possesses an impression which is shown in the exhibition.

We have not, however, finished with the work of Vertue, who was well acquainted with the features of Milton and is believed to have been scrupulously faithful in representing them. His fine folio print of 1725 is clearly taken from the Hobart and Bayfordbury portraits, probably from the former, and in the arrangement of hair, collar, cords and tassels follows the Hobart exactly, while in the softened expression of features it is more nearly like the Bayfordbury picture. He, however, invariably made one curious mistake. In Milton's arms was a double-headed eagle, but Vertue has always drawn it as a single-headed bird.

In addition to engraving portraits of the poet, Vertue made two drawings, both of which are in the author's collection. One is referred to on the plate engraved by W. N. Gardiner for the Boydell *Milton*, and this drawing is stated to have been at that time in the possession of Thomas Brand Hollis. From it is derived the engraving by Owen, and also to a certain extent those by Blood, Cooper, Hicks, Schmidt, and the one published in Pickering's 3 Vol. edition of the Poetical Works, 1826. It is possible that this drawing by Vertue was known to Van der Gucht when he executed his folio plate for Rolli's Italian translation of *Paradise Lost* in 1736, but while accepting the features, Van der Gucht, and those who followed him, Mollison and Baratti, have entirely transformed the costume, clothing the figure, to use Marsh's expressions, "in the slovenly undress in vogue among the artists of his day." The waistcoat, vest and collar are all represented open.

As regards collar and tassels this fine drawing by Vertue resembles the Hobart and Bayfordbury pictures, but the features are older in expression than in those portraits. The three French prints, 86, 87, 87*a*, are also taken from the Hobart picture in details, but in countenance resemble the Vertue drawing.

In the next group of prints we come again to the Bayfordbury picture, and the engravings by Miller, Simpson, Holl, Tallis, Dean and others, are all taken from the Bayfordbury portrait, and in fact several of them state in definite language that they are "from an original painting, by Faithorne, in the collection of William Bayford, Esq." As we have already stated this piece of information may be absolutely correct and the Bayfordbury drawing is most probably by Faithorne, but we cannot determine this with absolute certainty, as there is just a possibility that it is by Richardson, and a very indefinite possibility that it may be a unique large drawing by White. The general consensus of opinion, however, is strongly in favour of its being by Faithorne.

We now leave the engravings made from drawings and approach those derived from busts, medallions and seals.

Thomas Hollis, in a paper dated July 30, 1757, referred to an original model in clay of the head of Milton which he endeavoured to purchase, "but it was knocked down to Mr. Reynolds by a mistake of Mr. Ford the auctioneer." He goes on to state that two years before Mr. Vertue died, he had mentioned that he was the possessor of this bust, and that "he believed it was done by one Pierce," a sculptor whose bust of Wren can be seen in the Bodleian. Hollis' opinion, however, was that it was modelled by Abraham Simon, and that afterwards a seal was engraved after it, by his brother Thomas Simon. Reynolds gave £9. 12*s*. 0*d*. for the bust and sold it to Mr. Hollis for £12. 12*s*. 0*d*., and the original is now in the possession of Christ's College, Cambridge, and is illustrated in this book. From it more than one engraving has been made, the chief being the one which Richardson drew, and Vertue engraved, for the folio edition of Milton's Prose Works, 1738; and the one etched by Cipriani for Mr. Hollis, at the time that he owned the bust. In this latter etching (133) Cipriani has added a collar and buttoned vest to his own fancy. He also made another drawing of the same bust but this time in profile, and at the time he did it the bust had passed by will into the possession of Dr. Disney, Thomas Brand Hollis' successor in the estate. It was engraved by H. Meyer, see (114) and (114*a*). Now Richardson again comes on the scene, because he made a series of etchings from this bust, but clothed them in a collar with cords and tassels, exactly the same as he had done in his previous etchings, but altogether different from the square Genevan collar, which Cipriani and Vertue had put on to the bust. To these etchings he supplied a laurel wreath, differing in structure and in the number of leaves from the laurel wreaths used on (70) and (71), and added a quotation from *Mansus* below the bust and put the name of Milton in Greek letters on the pedestal. It will be seen therefore that, although he accepted the clay bust as his original model, he varied it considerably both in costume and in features to his own ideas. Not content, however, with this, he went still further, and produced a profile in 1738, to which he added the name of Milton in Greek letters, but this does not bear the very slightest resemblance to any other portrait of Milton in existence and is much more like Richardson himself or his own etching of Pope. Marsh believed that the original drawing for this etching belonged to Boswell and was sold at the sale of his library in 1825. Although intended for Milton it must not be accepted as a genuine portrait.

A far more interesting representation of the Christ's College bust is to be seen in the engraving made by Cipriani for Hollis (122), to commemorate Milton's victory over Salmasius. It was prepared to the design of Mr. Hollis and intended to illustrate a projected edition of Milton's Prose Works. Mr. Hollis paid Cipriani twenty-five guineas for it, but the edition of the Prose Works was never prepared, and the print appears in the memoirs of Hollis. There are two curious varieties of it (123) and (124).

From Rysbrack's monument in Westminster Abbey there are three prints, and from other busts three more, one of which (130), appearing as the frontispiece to Cowper's *Milton*, has no resemblance whatever to Milton. From medallions, there are six prints, the chief being the one which appears in Peck's memoirs and illustrates a medal struck at the expense of William Benson to be presented, as stated by Dr. Joseph Warton in a note to his brother's edition of the minor poems, for "the best verses that were produced on Milton at all our great schools." Of other medallions an interesting example is the one published by Sharpe in 1809, engraved by Smith, forming a vignette to the title page of the edition of *Paradise Lost*, 12mo, 1809.

Mr. Hollis is believed to have had a small steel puncheon of Milton's head, intended for a seal or ring, engraved by Thomas Simon, and Marsh states that this was afterwards in the possession of Mr. Albert Way. Simon certainly engraved a medallion for a seal of Milton, which is said to have been drawn by James Deacon, the miniature painter and wood engraver, who died in 1750. The seal belonged to Mr. Yeo, and Rylands made an engraving of it, which is now exceedingly rare. There are also three other engravings from this seal; on one the engraver's name could not be read by Mr. Marsh, who possessed the only known example of it, and the other two, almost equally precious, were engraved by Holloway and Romnery.

We now come to the large group of pretended portraits, chief amongst which is the miniature by Cooper. Its history is as follows. It was bought for one hundred guineas in 1784 by Sir Joshua Reynolds from a picture dealer named Hunt, who, according to Northcote, "had obtained it from a common furniture broker, who could not remember either the time or manner in which he came by it." It was signed with the painter's initials "S. C.," and dated 1653, and on the back of it was written the following inscription: "This picture belong'd to Deborah Milton who was her Fathers Amannuensis at her death was sold to Sr. Willm Davenants Family. It was painted by Mr. Saml Cooper who was painter to Oliver Cromwell at ye time Milton was Latin Secratary to ye Protector.—The Painter & Poet were near of the same age. Milton was born in 1608 & died in 1674. Cooper was born in 1609 & died in 1672 & were Companions & friends till Death parted Them. Several encouragers and Lovers of ye fine Arts at that time wanted this picture, particularly Lord Dorset John Somers Esqr Sr. Robt Howard Dryden Atterbury Dr. Aldrich & Sr. John Denham." In Warton's edition of *Milton*, 1784, the miniature was referred to, and in the second edition, 1791, again mentioned, with some additional remarks, suggesting that it resembled a portrait of Selden; and this statement gave rise to a letter in the *Gentleman's Magazine* of May 20th, 1791, written, so later facts proved, by Lord Hailes. Sir Joshua answered this letter on the 15th June, signing himself "R. J.," and his answer *in extenso* appears in Northcote's life. There was a further reply in the *Gentleman's Magazine* for October. Marsh sets forward, fairly clearly, the facts of the argument. Lord Hailes proved the impossibility of reconciling the statements given in the memorandum with the date of Deborah's death; pointed out that Sir John Denham died several years before Milton, and questioned the language used in the inscription and inferring that it would not have been in use at the time, and that the phrase "fine arts" was unknown in English until long after 1693. Sir Joshua endeavoured to meet his arguments, said that the memorandum was written before 1693, when Mr. Somers was knighted, and stated that as Milton died insolvent and Deborah Clarke was in great indigence, the portrait was sold by her to the author of the memorandum. Lord Hailes denied that Milton died insolvent, pointed out that Deborah was living apart from her father for several years before his death and was hardly likely, being so very poor, to have retained the miniature from 1674 to 1693 before she sold it. He also referred to her express statement to Vertue that "she knew of no other picture of her father than the two" in the possession of his widow. Sir Joshua Reynolds confined the greater part of his further argument to an opinion respecting the quality of the portrait, which was rather beside the mark, as its quality was unimpeachable, and the fact that it was a work of Cooper had never been called in question.

It is more now to the point to direct attention, to the fact, that the miniature does not resemble either of the accepted portraits, especially the one by Faithorne with which it has been compared. The President, however, strongly believed in its authenticity, and bequeathed it to the Reverend William Mason, who in his turn, by his will, in 1797, left it to William Burgh, Esq., LL.D., of York, and from him it passed into the possession of the Morritt family and has been preserved at Rokeby for many years. It is a very long time since the public have seen it, as Rokeby has been let many times and the miniature put away safely in the strong room, but when last it was exhibited in the early seventies, we had no hesitation in considering that, although an exceedingly fine miniature by Cooper, it bore no resemblance whatever to Milton. Curiously enough, however, it has been accepted by the public as the favourite portrait, has been engraved and reproduced many times, and still forms the frontispiece to one of the best editions of Milton's prose works, the Bohn edition, issued by George Bell and Sons. The story of the controversy appears on the plate engraved by Caroline Watson in 1786, and there are other representations of the portrait, both from her hand, in 1808, and from those of Boutrois, Haid, Cochran and Sharp, one of the best being the rare Sharp print, which was printed in Du Rouveray's edition of *Paradise Lost*, 1802, and again issued in 1808. Boutrois has curiously mixed up the whole story and has called the painter of the miniature Reynolds instead of Cooper. A very poor representation of the same miniature was drawn by W. M. Craig, but he has represented the poet full face, whereas the miniature is in profile. There are two impressions of his print known, both engraved by Hicks.

Another pretended portrait of the poet appeared in Peck's memoirs of Milton, in 1740. In a chapter on the portraits of the poet, page 103, in which the descriptions are mixed up in a most extraordinary way, Peck speaks of the one illustrated in his frontispiece as having belonged to Sir John Meres, of Kirby Belers in Leicestershire, and proceeds to describe the colouring of the original. His only reason for considering it to be a portrait of Milton is the fact that in the portrait a book is represented inscribed "Paradice Lost." Warton and Hollis were told that Peck asked Vertue whether he thought it a picture of Milton, and Vertue's reply was very emphatically in the negative, but Peck decided to have a mezzotint made of it and submitted to the public, and he did so. As Mr. Marsh states, "posterity has long since settled the difference, not much to Mr. Peck's credit," as "his effort was an impudent attempt to foist a pretended portrait upon the public." The portrait was issued separately from the volume, for sale to the public, and is therefore to be found in two states, one in black on the thin paper on which the book was printed, and another in a greenish black shade on rough, coarser and heavier paper with a very full margin.

Another miniature has been said to be a portrait of Milton. In January 1791, the Reverend J. Elderton, of Bath, referred in the *Gentleman's Magazine* to the existence of a miniature in his possession, which, he says, "belonged to his child's great ancestor, Sir Edward Seymour, who was Speaker of the House of Commons and grandfather of the Duke of Somerset: it has been seen by connoisseurs who always agreed it was an original: the hair is of a dark chestnut colour, flowing down to the shoulders." As some doubts were thrown upon its authenticity, Mr. Elderton forwarded an outline of the miniature to the *Magazine* and an engraving by Basire appeared in the issue for January, 1792. Its only resemblance to Milton consists in the long hair.

Another pretended portrait bears the name of Vertue and is dated 1751. It does not in the least resemble the authentic portraits, and was engraved by Vertue from a drawing which belonged to Richardson and was removed from his collection, he having died six years before. The person certainly has flowing hair and wears a gown and bands, but in no other respects resembles the poet.

Yet another portrait is declared as having been in the collection of Lord Chesterfield, and three different engravings are known of it. As regards the vest, gown and collar it has a slight resemblance to the Faithorne portrait, but it represents a young man with a moustache and long hair, leaning his head on his hand, in an attitude of thought, and there is no reason whatever to suppose it is in the least like the poet.

A still more absurd attempt to produce a portrait of Milton was made by Harding in 1796, but there is little doubt that his print represents Killigrew, and is after a picture by Vandyck, as explained in the details of the engraving (see (155)).

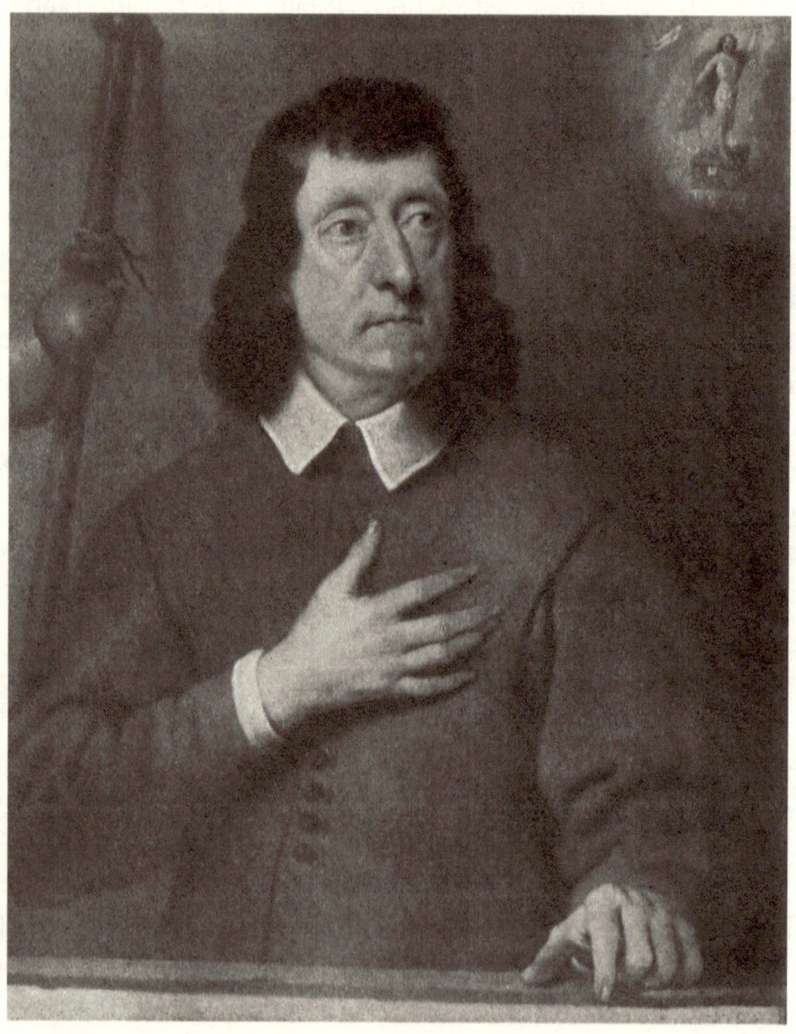

Portrait by Pieter van der Plas in the National Portrait Gallery considered to represent John Milton. See (156) and (157).

It is not quite so easy to dismiss off hand the picture of Milton by Pieter Van der Plas (see illustration). The original portrait hangs in the National Portrait Gallery, presented to the Trustees in 1839 by Mr. Capel Lofft, who always insisted that it was a portrait of Milton, and published it as such in his edition of *Paradise Lost*, Bury St. Edmunds, 1792. He said, it was bequeathed to his father, by Colonel Holland. The Director of the Portrait Gallery is by no means satisfied that it is a picture of Milton, and if it is by Pieter Van der Plas, as seems probable from the signature upon it, the doubt is intensified, because a Pieter van der Plas died in 1626, when Milton was but eighteen years old. There was, however, a Pieter David van der Plas who died in 1704, and the picture is probably by him. A staff and pilgrim's bottle and the representation of the risen Saviour would be, as Marsh points out, equally appropriate for Bunyan, whom the portrait certainly resembles, and a comparison with other portraits of Bunyan, notably the drawing in the British Museum by White, seems to us to make it more likely that the portrait is of the author of *Pilgrim's Progress* rather than of the author of *Paradise Lost*. It was, however, engraved by Quinton, as a portrait of Milton, and it was lithographed by M. Gauci, the lithograph being printed by F. Moser. The print is fairly common, except in an open letter proof, but the lithograph is exceedingly rare.

In Dr. Williams' Library, Gordon Square, is a picture by Dobson, a replica of which is in an important collection in New York, and it is possible that both the original and the replica are the work of the artist whose name they bear, but they have both been styled portraits of Milton, and an engraving by Wedgwood giving that information was issued in 1820. The portrait, however, represents a big, heavy man who bears no resemblance whatever to Milton. He has certainly a square collar with tassels, something like the one in the Faithorne drawing, but much later in date, has long hair and wears a buttoned vest and a gown, but there the resemblance ceases.

An even more absurd portrait is the one engraved by Charles Pye, 1823, which represents a young man of about twenty in the costume of 1710. To make it resemble the portraits of Milton it is declared to have been painted by Janssen, but it has no resemblance either to the work of Janssen or to the portraits of Milton. Yet another absurd portrait was engraved by R. Page.

We now refer to a miniature. A certain Mr. Falconer of Usk stated in *Notes and Queries* that he possessed a miniature, painted on vellum, which had belonged to his grandfather, and that it was the one from which an engraving was made, for the Society for the Diffusion of Useful Knowledge. He uses no particular arguments to connect the portrait with Milton, but declares that his miniature was by Faithorne. Faithorne, however, was not a miniature painter, and when Milton was of the age represented in this portrait Faithorne was a boy. The face is pleasing, but possesses little character, and the portrait is most certainly not the work of Faithorne nor representing Milton. It was very possibly a miniature and may have been dated 1667, but these are the only definite facts about it, and to claim it as a portrait of Milton, as has been claimed in many editions of the poet's works, is absurd. It is the favourite original from which busts both in stone and plaster were made, but it must not be regarded as authentic.

Another small portrait bears the inscription "From Faithorne," and slightly resembles the last-mentioned one, but the face is rounder and fuller and the hair is more curly. It was engraved by Smith, but is decidedly not a portrait of Milton and has not even any claim to be thought so.

There is a very poor engraving by Riedel which bears the name of Milton. It is a rough rendering of the original Faithorne print, very coarsely treated, and all the features of the poet's face have been lost.

Another, somewhat similar, was published in 1823 by G. Smeeton, and there again the features have been so changed that no resemblance in them to Milton's original appearance can be traced.

The two lithographs, the one by Schubert and the other by Marckl, representing blind men, and the print by Maulet published in Paris, probably have no claim to be considered as anything more than fancy likenesses of the blind poet, but they bear his name and therefore must be alluded to, although they do not in the least resemble him.

There is a very tiny rectangular line engraving also called Milton, very freely adapted from the Faithorne print, so freely as to have little or no connection with the poet: and finally a full length portrait, engraved by Fougeron, is declared to represent Milton and is not in the least like him in any respect.

A very rare print, 8vo in size, mentioned in Rodd's *Catalogue of British Portraits*, 1812, was alluded to by Marsh, but he had never seen a copy of it. We have it in two states and in two inks, in our collection, and it is a good piece of engraving after the Faithorne print, but very much reduced. It bears the signature G. Coster, sculpt., and has below the portrait Dryden's well-known lines, but engraved in script. In our own time C. W. Sherborn has made a clever etching to which he has given the name of Milton. The etching resembles to a certain extent the miniature bearing the name of Milton and belonging to the collection of the Duke of Buccleuch and Queensberry, and is said to have been taken from it. It is not, however, exactly the same as that miniature, the artist having taken considerable licence both with the features, which he has made far older than those in the miniature, and with the white collar and costume.

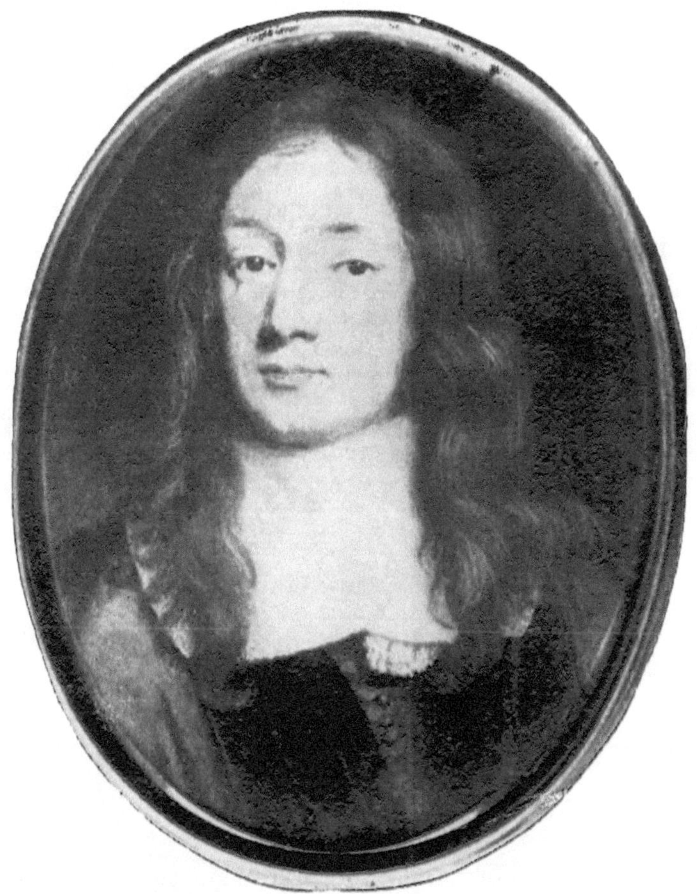

Miniature by Samuel Cooper, belonging to the Duke of Buccleuch and Queensberry, said to represent John Milton as a young man. See under Portraits.

Two other prints, named by Marsh but not seen or described by him, are as follows. A 4to print of Milton at four ages, representing the Janssen,

Onslow, Hollis and Vertue portraits engraved by Joh. H. Lips, 1779, and the print by Hollar referred to by Parthey. This latter is certainly by W. Hollar, but almost as certainly not Milton. It represents a bust of a very young man, is unlettered and of extreme rarity.

Wivell refers to a Faber print of Milton on a sheet with Shakespeare, Jonson and Butler, but this we have not seen, and Marsh had heard of a rare 12mo print by Phinn and a folio by Gunst but had not seen either of them.

It will now be well to refer in conclusion to certain other portraits said to represent Milton. In the exhibition at South Kensington in 1866 there were two pictures exhibited by the Countess De La Warr, one, said to be the work of Jonathan Richardson, and with an open untidy costume, a little like that of Van der Gucht's engraving. The features are not, however, identical, and the collar, which is quite plain in the engraving, was fringed with lace in the De La Warr picture. It was a portrait on canvas, 37 inches by 28 inches, but it cannot be seriously contended that it represented Milton. The other picture was by Mary Beale, although attributed to Richardson. It measured 20 inches by 15 inches, and is of a young man with long reddish hair, but is not a portrait of Milton. These portraits are now at Knole, Sevenoaks. At the same exhibition there was shown by the Reverend R. C. Jenkins a portrait of a man in dark dress with a square cut white collar and tassels and with long hair, dated 1650 and inscribed Age 42. It was on canvas, 27 inches by 23 inches, and although it certainly bears some slight resemblance to the Faithorne engraving, yet the resemblance is not sufficient for us to claim it as an authentic portrait. There is a third portrait at Knole, also said to represent Milton. It is in *grisaille*, 7 feet 1 inch by 4 feet 10 inches, and perhaps the work of De Wit. It represents a bust of the poet within a niche, having at the base some clever floral decoration. All three pictures Lord Sackville has been good enough to lend to Christ's College.

The oil painting in the hall of Christ's College, see illustration, represents a boy of a pleasing, sweet countenance, and it has a certain amount of resemblance to the early portrait of John Milton and some slight connection with the Onslow portrait. Its history, before Mr. Hildyard bought it, is not known, but it has always borne the name of Milton, and it is quite possible that it is a portrait of the poet as a boy.

The miniature at Montagu House, see illustration, is certainly a work by Cooper and a very delightful one. It is a signed work originally belonging to a

Mr. Villiers, of Tours, and was sold as a portrait of Milton by Messrs Foster, the auctioneers, at a general sale of the Villiers property. We believe that Michael Bryan was the first person to pronounce it to be a portrait of Milton, and upon what authority he did so we do not know. Probably it was only on the general resemblance which it bore to the Onslow portrait as shown in the Houbraken engraving. It is quite possible that it may represent the poet, but we have no particular evidence to support the contention and are inclined to think that it has been called a portrait of Milton more because it represents a young man with long hair who wears a buttoned vest, a broad white collar, and has tassels showing below the margin of the collar. The presence, however, of two broad bands of black velvet down the front of the gown leads us to fear that the attribution is in error. Somewhat similar velvet appears on the Cooper-Reynolds miniature (141), but there is no reason to suppose that Milton had any velvet on his usual costume.

There were some miniatures bearing the name of John Milton exhibited at South Kensington Museum in 1865. Mr. J. G. Fanshawe lent a portrait painted in oil which he attributed to Samuel Cooper (520), Mr. C. Sackville Bale a pencil drawing on paper (1801) by Richardson, closely resembling the Richardson etching already referred to. It had four portrait heads on one sheet, the central one representing John Milton and the other three Alexander Pope. The sheet had been prepared for Horace Walpole, and each drawing was signed at the back by Richardson. It came from the Strawberry Hill collection. Mr. T. M. Whitehead lent an enamel on gold representing the poet when young, and attributed to Petitot, and Mr. W. Phillipps lent an oil portrait which be ascribed to Samuel Cooper.

The last-named item is believed to have passed into the collection of the late Dr. Propert and to have been sold in May 1897 to Mr. Vernon Watney, but neither of the other exhibits can now be traced. It would be most interesting to find the Richardson drawing and compare it with the etchings by that painter now brought together. In the Victoria and Albert Museum there is an enamel copy of the Janssen portrait by Wm Essex, signed and dated 1856, and another fine enamel portrait of the poet belongs to Mr. J. W. Whitehead.

Finally, we would make a brief mention of the last portrait of the poet which has been discovered, and which belongs to the author. Its history is that it was acquired from a member of the Goddard family, and that the mother of its late owner was a Miss Woodcock, who stated that the portrait had always been in the Woodcock family and had been handed down in direct succession from Catherine Woodcock, whom Milton married on November 12th, 1656. This Catherine Woodcock was the daughter of a Captain Woodcock of Hackney, and the Woodcocks who owned the miniature stated that their home was in Hackney. The second Mrs. Milton had a baby girl on October 19th, 1657, and both she and the child died in February, 1658, and the miniature was bequeathed to Catherine Woodcock's niece, from thence coming, it is stated, in direct succession down to its late owner. It is of course quite conceivable that Deborah Milton should have known nothing whatever of any portrait of her father which had belonged to his second wife, whom she knew for so short a time; and it can be readily understood that if, as surmised, this portrait was given to his wife, by the poet, it would be retained by her descendants, and would not fall into the hands either of the children of the first wife or of his widow, who was the third. It appears to have been cherished very tenderly by the people to whom it belonged, and their descendants only parted with it when actually compelled so to do. It is specially interesting, if a portrait of Milton, as it represents the poet at a period of his life at which we have no other portrait, for he was sixty-two when Faithorne made his engraving, and this miniature must have been painted when he was about forty-eight. It is also of peculiar importance because on two occasions Aubrey speaks of the colour of Milton's hair in middle life, once calling it "light brown," and on another occasion "reddish." Towards the end of his life this colour disappeared, but is clearly shown in the miniature in question. Aubrey also speaks of his complexion as "exceeding fayre," says that his face was "oval" and that he was "a spare man," and all these characteristics and the somewhat more elaborate detail of the lace collar worn at that special time agree with what is to be seen in this miniature. There is certainly a distinct resemblance to Milton in the miniature, and the pedigree gives it some special importance. It does not appear to have been the subject of any engraving, which is perhaps natural owing to the special history belonging to it. It has been attributed to Edmund Ashfield, but on this point we have no very definite theory. It is certainly, however, a genuine miniature of about the middle of the 17th century, bearing a very strong resemblance to Milton and

having come from a family from amongst whose members Milton selected
the second wife, who was only spared to him for the short period of fifteen
months.

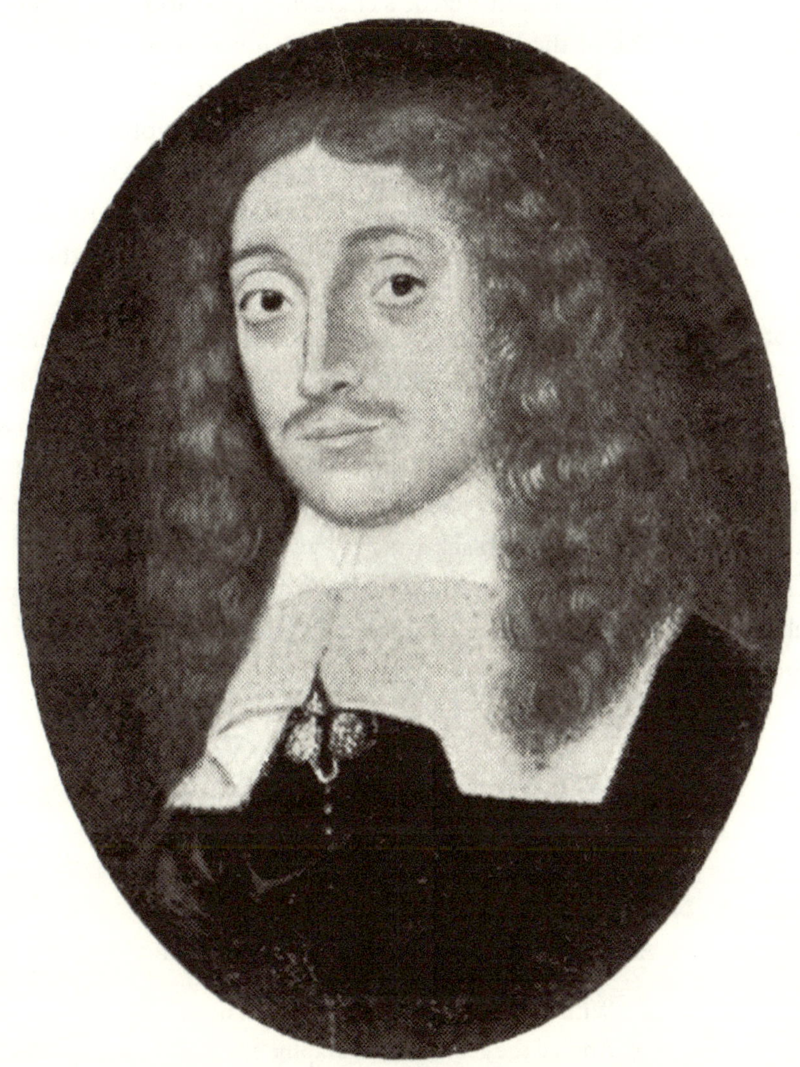

John Milton when about 48. The Woodcock portrait.
In the collection of Dr. G. C. Williamson.

The two portrait drawings of Milton already briefly mentioned are both
the work of George Vertue and in the possession of the author of this
catalogue. One of them appears likely to have been the original drawing in

stump and wash for the engraving made in 1747, and closely resembles the portrait in that engraving (34) in all the details of costume, but the countenance is smoother and more refined in the drawing than as completed in the print. The expression in Vertue's engravings (33) and (34) differs very much from the look of the Faithorne print, which we know was taken from life, and the engraver lost much of the rugged stern expression of the poet and rendered the face smoother and more benignant than Faithorne had made it. This process of softening, however, is carried to a still further extent by Vertue in the drawing now under consideration, and in it the face has lost almost all its stern, forcible expression, and remains a quiet, smooth, thoughtful countenance, which may perhaps be that of an ideal Milton but is not that of Faithorne's print. The drawing in question was originally at Strawberry Hill and came from the Walpole, Woodburn and William Pearce collections, and has the book plate of the last named collector on its reverse. It is inscribed on the back, however, in 18th century handwriting, as having come originally from the collection of "Thurlow, Secretary to Oliver Cromwell," and to have been drawn by "G. V." It is in black and grey wash. H. 7. W. 8.

The other drawing by Vertue also came from Strawberry Hill and has attached to it a note in Horace Walpole's handwriting respecting Vertue, reading as follows:

THE EPITAPH.

Here lyes the body of George Vertue
late Engraver
And fellow of the Society of Antiquaries,
Who was born in London anno 1684
And departed this life on the 24th of July 1756.

With manners gentle and a grateful heart
And all the genius of the graphic art;
His fame shall each succeeding artist own
Longer by far than monuments of stone.

"Vertue was a rigid Roman Catholic, & ordered his body to be buried in the Cloysters of Westminster Abbey, as near as possible to a spot where he had found a monk of his name had anciently been buried."

It is a far more important drawing than the last, as it is undoubtedly the original by Vertue for print No. 79, where the inscription records that the engraving by W. N. Gardiner is taken from "an original drawing by Vertue in the collection of Thomas Brand Hollis, Esq., at the Hyde, Essex." This drawing is on canvas, in black and brown wash, and is a little larger than the print, measuring 7¼ in height and 6⅛ in width, sight sizes, whereas the print is only 6 in height and 4¾ in width. A proof impression of this print is in the author's collection, evidently struck off before the outer ruling of the plate was made and before any inscription was engraved upon it, and if anything this proof impression more closely resembles the drawing than does the finished plate. This drawing appears to have passed from Strawberry Hill into the possession of Mr. Hollis, and from him came to Dr. Disney, a member of whose family sold it a few years since.

Of attributed portraits there are many. A full-faced portrait on panel 17½ by 14½, is at the Holburne Art Museum, Bath, another is stated to be in the Examination Hall of Queen's College, Belfast, and there are two within the walls of Christ's College, one in the Hall and the other in the possession of Mr. Arthur Shipley. A curious one bearing Milton's arms and name belongs to Mrs. Morrison of St. Albans, and is clearly based on the Richardson etchings, and there are portraits belonging to Lord Leconfield and other owners. Fuller details of many of them will be found further on.

G. C. W.

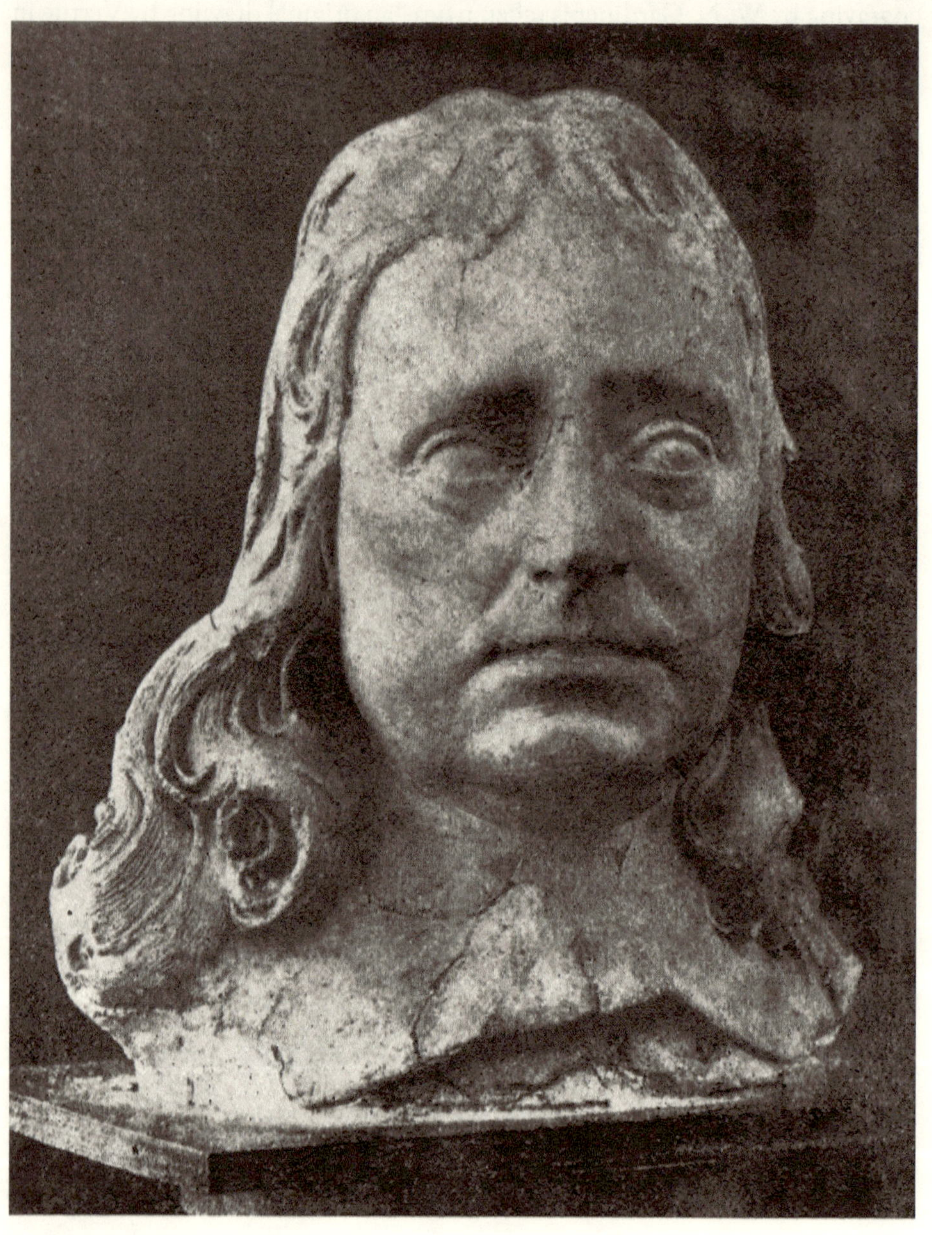

The Clay bust of Milton, said to be the work of Pierce, now preserved in the Library of Christ's College, Cambridge. See under Statuary.

CATALOGUE OF THE PORTRAITS OF JOHN MILTON

STATUARY WORK

1. Clay bust.

Lent by Christ's College, Cambridge. The following is a copy of a letter
respecting this bust written by Mr. Aldis Wright to Dr. Cartmell, Master
of Christ's College, 1849-1881.

TRINITY COLLEGE,
CAMBRIDGE.

13 *Nov.* 1875.

MY DEAR MASTER OF CHRIST'S,

Since I had the pleasure, thanks to your kindness, of seeing the Milton Bust in
company with Mr. and Mrs. Woolner, I have learnt some particulars about it
which I think will be interesting to you.

In the life of Thomas Hollis (4° London, 1870) Vol. II. p. 513 there is an
engraving by Cipriani, as unlike the original as anything can well be, which is said
to be 'from a bust in plaister modelled from the life now in the possession of
Thomas Hollis.' The engraving is dated 1760.

I now transcribe what is said of the bust itself. "Mr. Hollis, in a paper dated
July 30, 1757, says, 'For an original model in clay of the head of Milton, £9. 12*s.*
which I intended to have purchased myself, had it not been knocked down to Mr.
Reynolds by a mistake of Mr. Ford the auctioneer.'

"Note, about two years before Mr. Vertue died, he told me, that he had been
possessed of this head many years; and that he believed it was done by one Pierce,
a sculptor of good reputation in those times the same who made the bust in
marble of Sir Christopher Wren, which is in the Bodleian Library. My own
impression is, that it was modelled by Abraham Simon; and that afterwards a seal
was engraved after it, in profile, by his brother Thomas Simon, a proof impression
of which is now in the hands of Mr. Yeo engraver in Covent Garden. This head
was badly designed by Mr. Richardson, and then engraved by Mr. Vertue, and
prefixed to Milton's prose-works, in quarto, printed for A. Millar, 1753 (Barons
edition). The bust probably was executed soon after Milton had written his

'Defensio pro "populo Anglicano.' Mr. Reynolds obligingly parted with this bust to Mr. Hollis for twelve guineas."

Vertue whose seal is mentioned, was the engraver who died in 1756. Who Mr. Reynolds may have been I can only conjecture. Perhaps Sir Joshua.

Believe me, my dear Master,

Yours very sincerely,

W. ALDIS WRIGHT.

THE REV.

    THE MASTER OF CHRIST'S.

2. Mr Horace Montford's original model for the statue at St. Giles Cripplegate (1904) is to be seen in the vestibule to the College Chapel. A photograph of it is exhibited.

Full length, rectangular. Full face, slightly to the right, long hair, long buttoned coat, the lower buttons being unfastened, white turned down collar with tasselled ends of cord appearing below, sleeves with buttons down the inside of the arm, knee breeches with bows, broad shoes with high tongues and bows, wide soft felt hat in left hand, fingers of gloves appearing from right-hand pocket of coat. Stands on small round pedestal. H. 8⅛. W. 4.

3. Marble bust of the head only, by Horace Montford, see 1. Lent by Christ's College, Cambridge. Removed from the Hall.

4. A replica of the above in plaster. Lent by Arthur E. Shipley, Esq., F.R.S.

5. Bronze miniature replica of the full length statue, see 1. Lent by Arthur E. Shipley, Esq., F.R.S.

6. Stone Bust inscribed: J. M. Bloomfield, Paddington. The ordinary unauthentic representation of the poet. Lent by Christ's College, Cambridge.

7. A similar smaller bust. Lent by Christ's College, Cambridge.

8. Derby Biscuit Bust, modelled by G. Cooper and acquired from his grandson. Rare. From the Faithorne portrait. Lent by Dr. Williamson.

9. Robinson and Leadbetter's Parian Bust. Lent by Dr. Williamson.

10. Wedgwood's Black Basalt Bust. Lent by Dr. Williamson.

11. Old Staffordshire Bust. Lent by Dr. Williamson.

12. Wedgwood's Bust in Basalt. Lent by Arthur E. Shipley, Esq., F.R.S.

13. Plaster Bust. Lent by A.E. Shipley, Esq. F.R.S.

14.

15.

16. Probably the work of a member of the Lens family. Lent by Arthur E. Shipley, Esq., F.R.S.

Three-quarter face to the right. Boyish expression, blue buttoned doublet, falling lace ruff showing two tassels, long hair, brown background.

Oval, 2¼ by 2¾. Acacia wood frame.

This miniature almost exactly resembles the Houbraken engraving dated 1741, and it has been suggested, with some degree of probability, that it was prepared in order to send to Houbraken, in Amsterdam, that from it he might engrave his plate. Such a course was often pursued with regard to original works. It was very possibly painted by Bernard Lens the younger. It is not an exact copy of the Nuneham portrait, which purports to be an absolute copy of the lost Onslow portrait. In costume the two are identical, but in expression of countenance they are not, although the miniature is identical with the engraving. It came from the collection of Mr. W. S. Green of Exeter Mansions, Shaftesbury Avenue, and was purchased by its present owner in 1903. It may of course be a copy by a miniature painter, from the Houbraken engraving; especially as the colour of the costume differs from that of the Nuneham portrait, where the coat is black while in the miniature it is blue; but it is suggested that the first suggestion is more likely to be the correct one.

17. ARTIST UNKNOWN. Lent by Dr. Williamson.

Three-quarter face to the left. Costume, black buttoned vest, black gown, square white collar with broad lace border tied with strings and showing the two tassels below. Long fair hair, very pallid countenance, brown background.

Oval, 1¾ by 2¼. Metal frame.

This portrait came from the Goddard family, who had received it in direct descent through Mrs. Goddard (born Elizabeth Woodcock), from Milton's second wife, Catherine Woodcock, the daughter of Captain Woodcock of Hackney whom the poet married on November 12th, 1656, and to whom he is said to have given this portrait. Mrs. Milton died in February, 1658, and the portrait was given by her to her niece, from whom it came to its late owners.

18. ARTIST UNKNOWN. Lent by Dr. Williamson.

Three-quarter face slightly to the right. Black buttoned vest, black gown, plain
white collar tied with strings and showing the strings and the two tassels,
long brown hair, background dark blue.

Oval, 2¼ by 2¾. Metal frame.

This is identical with the engraving by George Vertue dated 1725. It was
originally in the possession of Charles Kean who regarded it as an early 18th
century copy and who framed it, together with two similar copies of engravings
representing Shakespeare and Jonson, which he obtained at the same time.

19. ARTIST UNKNOWN, probably Essex. Lent by J. W. Whitehead, Esq.

Enamel. The Onslow portrait. Inscribed: "J. Milton ann ætatis (*not very
clearly written*) suæ 20 C. J. fecit 1627." H. 4. W. 3. Black spotted vest,
boyish face. This is a curious enamel because it ascribes to C. Janssen the
Onslow portrait which he is not supposed to have painted, and has
confused it with the early portrait which he did paint. The Onslow portrait
was of Milton when 21. This states when 20, and the words anno or ætatis
are written by some one not conversant with either word and are mingled
up together in a strange confusion.

It is a good example of the mistakes so constantly made with regard to the
portraits of Milton.

PORTRAITS

20. BENJAMIN VAN DER GUCHT. Lent by the Right Honourable Lewis
Harcourt, M.P.

Bust, slightly to the right, the head turned towards the spectator. Fair hair falling
to neck, boyish expression, falling ruff, black dress, brown background.

Canvas 28½ by 24½. Oval.

The following inscription is upon the back of the picture:

This original picture of Milton I bought in the year 1729 or 30 and paid 20
guineas for it of Mr. Cumberbatch, a gentleman of very good consideration in
Chester, who was a relation and executor of the will of Milton's last wife who died
a little while before that time. He told me it hung up in her chamber till her death

and she used to say that her husband gave it to her to show her what he was in his youth being drawn when he was about 21 years of age.

AR. ONSLOW.

Mr. Hawkins Brown (author of the poem De Animi Immortalitate) told me (8 Oct. 1753) that he knew this Mrs. Milton, visited her often and well remembered this picture hanging in her chamber which she said was her husband.

A. O.

Compare this picture with that of Milton in his old age or in the print of it by White.

N. B. The above I transcribed from the writings I found on the back of the original picture of Milton belonging to Lord Onslow when I made this copy for the Earl of Harcourt in November 1792.

BENJ. VAN DER GUCHT.

"Lord Onslow and Lord Harcourt were great friends and both fond of art. They made an agreement towards the end of the last century to exchange copies of two pictures

1. Milton,

2. Pope by Kneller,

the latter belonging to Lord Harcourt. The faithful copies were made and exchanged. Since that date the original Onslow picture has been lost and no search through every gallery and known locality has ever been able to trace it, and therefore Lord Harcourt claimed to possess the only known copy from the picture and the next best thing to the original, which Lord Onslow had never before allowed to be copied."

This picture was exhibited at the Oxford Exhibition of Historical Portraits in 1905, No. 115, and was illustrated in the catalogue.

21. Artist probably FAITHORNE. The Bayfordbury picture. Lent by H. Clinton Baker, Esq.

Crayon drawing, ? inches by ? inches. See illustration.

22. ARTIST UNKNOWN. Lent by Christ's College, Cambridge.

Oil painting on canvas.

Boyish face, long hair, lace collar, black coat. Nothing is known of the history of this portrait save that it was purchased in the middle of the 19th century by the Rev. J. Hildyard, Rector of Ingoldsby and at one time Fellow and

Tutor of the College, as a portrait of Milton as a young man. It has always borne that name and is merely accepted as a possible representation of the poet in his youth.

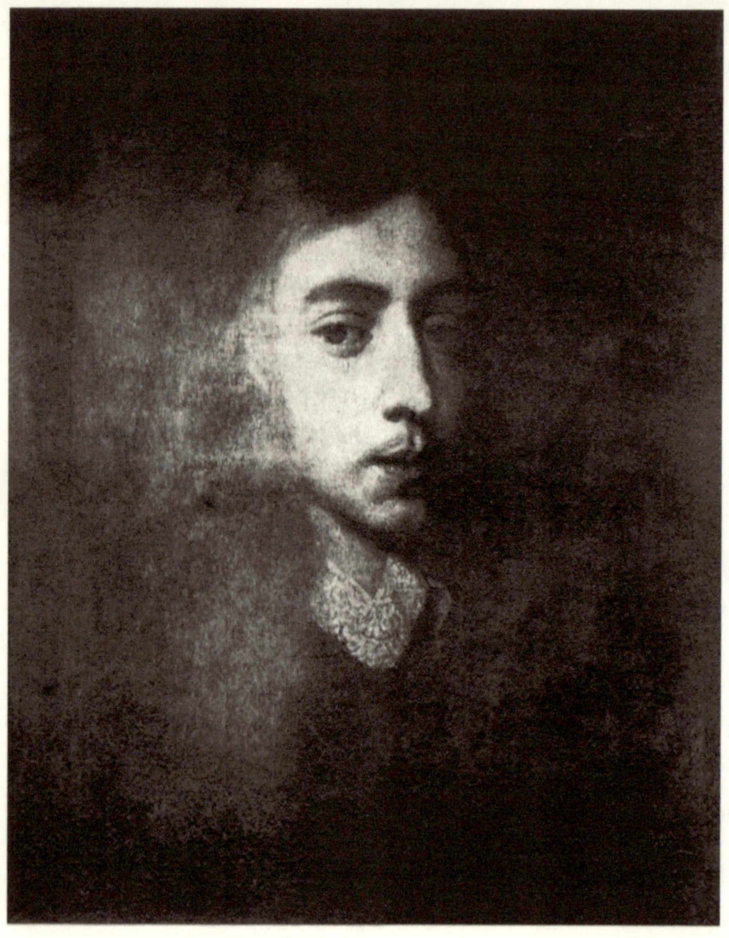

Milton a young man. The oil painting in the Hall of Christ's College, Cambridge.
See under Portraits.

23. ARTIST UNKNOWN. Lent by Arthur E. Shipley, Esq., F.R.S.
Oil painting on an elaborately constructed mahogany panel. Measurements over all 2 ft. 11 in. by 2 ft. 5 in. Boyish face, black coat, white tie, long hair, white vest revealed in front.

This picture came from Miss Elizabeth Rider (or Ryther) of the White House, Kirby Wiske, Yorkshire, the house in which the famous Roger Ascham was born, and for a long time hung in the room in which the great scholar first saw the light. Miss Rider's statement respecting it is as follows:

"In Cromwell's days, when Milton was the secretary of the Protector my ancestor, Sir John Ryther of Rider Hall (or Ryder), was one of the gentlemen of the court and a personal friend of the poet. I believe that it was by his desire that the portrait was painted but whether he had it painted or purchased it directly afterwards I do not know, but it has always been regarded by the family as an authentic portrait."

It was purchased by the owner on the death of Miss Rider, through Mr. John Rigby of Altrincham.

24. MARY BEALE. Lent by Lord Sackville.
Bust looking to the right, brown dress, open collar, long reddish hair. Canvas
   19 inches by 15 inches.

25. JONATHAN RICHARDSON. Lent by Lord Sackville.
Open collar, yellowish open vest, cloak held by left hand. Canvas 37 inches by
   28 inches.

26. Possibly DE WIT. Lent by Lord Sackville.
Representation in *grisaille*, of a bust of Milton standing in a niche, with floral
   ornamentation below. The poet wears the "Faithorne" collar with tassels.
   Canvas 7 feet 1 inch by 4 feet 10 inches.

27. ARTIST UNKNOWN. Lent by Mrs. Morrison.
Face to the right, long hair, plain white collar tied with cord and fastened by
   two tassels, black buttoned vest, black gown. Canvas 30½ by 24½ inches.
The head is crowned with a wreath of laurel. Inscribed: "Joannis Miltoni,"
   and having upon it the Milton arms in a shield. This is said to have been
   painted by Milton himself but there is no evidence whatever to support the
   assertion. The portrait resembles the Richardson etchings to a certain
   extent and the Faithorne engraving in costume but the features are very
   little like those of Milton and the expression far too smooth for his.
It cannot be accepted as an original likeness of the poet and is probably a
   composition based upon the Richardson etchings.
See Antiquarian Magazine, vol. II. 1882, page 1.

28. ARTIST UNKNOWN. Lent by Lord Leconfield.

29. ARTIST UNKNOWN. Lent by Dr. Hill, some time Master of Downing College.

Portrait of Milton, ætat 31, from the collection of Mr. Peed of Canterbury, a collector of Miltoniana who died about 1820.

30. CORNELIS JANSSEN. Lent by J. Passmore Edwards, Esq.

Portrait of Milton at the age of 10; see page 5 and page 131, and *The* Times of 3 June, 1908.

30a. ROBERT WALKER. Lent by Rev. C. P. Jones, of Buntingford.

30b. VAN DER PLAS. Lent by the Trustees of the National Portrait Gallery, by permission of the Treasury.

30c. ARTIST UNKNOWN. Lent by Major Galton of Hadzor.

30d. ARTIST UNKNOWN. Lent by E. Garnett, Esq., of Horsforth.

30e. ARTIST UNKNOWN. Photograph of the portrait in the Dyce collection at the Victoria and Albert Museum, inscribed: "John Milton, Esq. Done after the life 1658, aet. 50." The original is said to have come down in the family of Bargrave, Chaplain to Charles I, and the portrait is evidently that of Milton, and has a close resemblance to the Faithorne engraving, from which it is probably derived.

30f. SAMUEL COOPER. Photograph of the miniature in the Victoria and Albert Museum.

The miniature is certainly the work of Cooper, but it cannot be accepted as a portrait of Milton.

30g. ARTIST UNKNOWN. Lent by Mr. W. Webber.

This has been called a portrait of Milton from a slight resemblance it bears to the Onslow portrait, but it cannot be accepted as an authentic likeness.

N.B. The author of this catalogue can only accept as genuine contemporary portraits of Milton, the Passmore Edwards portrait (30), the Onslow portrait (20), and the Bayfordbury drawing (21), although he is disposed to accept the Woodcock miniature (17) as a contemporary work, and there is no doubt that the Vertue drawing, although not *ad vivum*, has high claim to be considered an authentic likeness of the poet, and one closely resembling the Bayfordbury portrait. He is disposed to think that the Dyce portrait (30e) is early and important, but not a contemporary portrait, while all the others must be considered as unauthentic, or as compositions derived from engravings, or from the imagination of the respective artists.

The Hobart drawing, generally accepted as a contemporary portrait, and the work of Faithorne, has not been lent to the Exhibition. It has therefore been impossible to compare it with the Bayfordbury drawing, as was desired, and to decide upon its merits. It is, however, a very important drawing, although there are diverse opinions as to its being the work of Faithorne, and it probably ranks next in position to the Bayfordbury drawing. Closer examination of it may perhaps result in its receiving an even higher position than is thus stated, and it may eventually be decided that it is the more trustworthy of the two drawings, but at present, without the opportunity of comparison, the opinion of the author cannot be more definitely stated.

It seems to be quite clear that the Richardson etchings, without the *laurel wreath*, are copied direct from the Bayfordbury drawing, which may, therefore, at one time have been in Richardson's possession.

DRAWINGS

31. GEORGE VERTUE. Drawing in stump and wash described on page 31.
7 inches by 8 inches. Lent by Dr Williamson.

32. GEORGE VERTUE. Drawing on canvas in black and brown wash described on page 33.
7¼ inches by 6⅛ inches. Lent by Dr. Williamson.

32a. J. B. CIPRIANI.
In the Fitzwilliam Museum (Portfolio 505) is the original drawing for engraving 137. It was presented to the Right Hon. Arthur Onslow by Mr. Thomas Hollis, and by Mr. (afterwards Lord) Onslow given to Lord Fitzwilliam, "at Richmond on Thursday, 25 Feb. 1790." The inscription upon it records that it was "drawn from a bust in plaister, modelled from, *and big as* life," differing from the inscription on the print by the addition of the words in italics. The inscription also includes a sentence from Petrarch:

Che trae buoni del sepolcro e in vita il scriba,

and on the drawing itself, which is in chalk, are the words:

By Deeds of Peace.

The drawing is a very beautiful one.

ENGRAVINGS, MEZZOTINTS, ETCHINGS AND LITHOGRAPHS

N.B. The numbers in brackets refer to the list prepared by J. F. Marsh in May, 1860, for his article on the Portraits of Milton for the Historic Society of Lancashire and Cheshire; see Vol. XII. page 135. The numbers that have a, b, or c added to them *and which are not in brackets* refer to prints unknown to Marsh and discovered since the date of his article. The whole of his list is given for reference, and heavier numbers are supplied to the prints exhibited in this exhibition. It will be understood that those which have *not* these heavier numbers attached, are prints which it has not been found possible to acquire or to borrow. In some instances they are exceedingly scarce and examples of them only occur in the public museums. In the sizes of the prints the height is given first, H. signifying the entire height or height of plate, P.H. portrait height, W. width, P.W. portrait width.

Of the prints exhibited Nos. 48, 52, 69, 76, 78, 107, and 117 are lent by Arthur E. Shipley, Esq., F.R.S.; all the remainder are from the collection of Dr G. C. Williamson.

ENGRAVINGS DERIVED FROM JANSSEN'S PORTRAIT

33. J. B. CIPRIANI, engraver.

(1) Half length in oval. ¾ face to the right. Short hair, striped doublet, buttoned in front and ornamented at shoulders, white stiffened lace collar showing Ioops of cord and tassels at throat. The oval is surrounded by a wreath of rose buds and leaves. Inscribed:

JOHN MILTON.

Drawn and etched MDCCLX by I. B. Cipriani a Tvscan from a pictvre painted by Cornelivs Iohnson MDCXVIII now in the possession of Thomas Hollis of Lincoln's Inne F.R. and A.S.S.

When **I** was yet a child no childish play
To me was pleasing all my mind was set

Seriovs to learn and know and thence to do
What might be public good my self I thovght
Born to that end born to promote all trvth
All righteovs things.

Parad. Reg.

H. 10⅝. P.H. 6. W. 6⅞. P.W. 4⅜.
Below the portrait is the Hollis Cap of Liberty.
Mentioned by Bromley.

34. CORNELIUS JANSEN *pinxit.* W. N. GARDINER, *sculpt.*
(**2**) Nearly full face. Short hair parted right and left, stiff lace collar, striped tightly fitting buttoned doublet. Inscribed:

John Milton.
Ætat 10.

From an Original Picture in the Collection of Thos. Brand Hollis, Esq., near the Hyde, Essex. Published, June 4, 1794, by John and Josiah Boydell and George Nicol.
H. 10½. P.H. 4¼. W. 7¼. P.W. 3.
This appeared in Boydell's *Milton*, 3 vols. royal folio.

35. ANON. *engraver.*
2a. Line engraving in an oval, representing the head and bust only, similar to the last. At the foot of the oval are printed the words "John Milton at the age of ten."
H. 2¾. P.H. 2½. W. 2. P.W. 1⅞.

36. EDWARD RADCLYFFE, *engraver.*
(**3**) A line engraving forming one of the illustrations to the first volume of Masson's *Life of Milton.* Inscribed "Milton Ætat 10. After a photograph from the original picture in the possession of Edgar Disney of the Hyde, Ingatestone, Essex. London. Published by Macmillan & Co. 1874."

37. ANON. *engraver.*
(**4**) Engraving of a boy's portrait, almost in outline. Buttoned vest, rich pendant lace collar. Inscribed.
Portrait described in *Gent. Mag.* for Sept. 1787, p. 759.
H. 7½. W. 4¾.

This was used to illustrate a letter signed Z. Z. dated from Oxford and sending the drawing from which this was engraved. The correspondent stated that the drawing had at the top "A O 1623 Ætat suae 12" and that in the hands of the figure was a book with "Homer's Iliad" on the leaves.

Engravings after the Onslow Portrait

(**5**) Granger refers to a print differing only from (**6**) in the inscription. Bromley also mentions it, but Marsh did not see any copy of it. Stated to be inscribed as follows: "Joannes Milton. Ætat. 21. Vertue, sc. Ex pictura archetypa quae penes est praehonorabilem Arthurum Onslow, Arm. Vertue sc. 1831." It is a quarto print.

38. G. VERTUE, *sculpt.* 1731.

(**6**) Half-length in oval. Three-quarter face to the right. Hair fairly long, doublet buttoned in front and ornamented at the shoulders, white lace ruff. The oval is in a rectangular frame which cuts the curve at the sides and top. At the top is a scroll ornament with leaves and flowers. On the edge of the frame at the foot is a ribbon bearing the words "Ioannes Milton." Below the frame is a stone shelf with the heads of Homer and Virgil: in the centre is a medallion with a single headed eagle; hanging from the shelf on either side below this medallion is a ribbon with the inscription "Ætatis XXI." Below the shelf is inscribed:

Nascuntur Poetae, non fiunt.

H. 9⅝. P.H. 4¾. W. 6¾. P.W. 4.

Published in Bentley's edition of Paradise Lost. 4to. London, 1732. Mentioned by Bromley.

39. ANON. but clearly the same plate as **6** with altered inscription.

6a. Half length in oval. Three-quarter face to the right. Hair fairly long, doublet buttoned in front and ornamented at the shoulders, white lace ruff. The oval is in a rectangular frame which cuts the curve at the sides and top. At the top is a scroll ornament with leaves and flowers. On the edge of the frame at the foot is a ribbon bearing the words "Ioannes Milton." Below the frame is a stone shelf with the head of Homer on it

46

and the head of Virgil: in the centre is a medallion with a single headed
eagle; hanging from the shelf on either side below this medallion is a
ribbon with the words "Ætatis suæ 21." Below the shelf is inscribed:

Græcia Mæonidem jactet sibi Roma Maronem
Anglia Miltonum jactat utrique parem. Selvaggi.

H.8¾. P.H. 4¾. W. 6. P.W. 4.

40. (**7**) & **7**a. There is a print from the same plate as (**6**) and **6**a with Dryden's
lines substituted for the "Nascuntur" etc., and the date badly altered from
1731 to 1747. It is prefixed to Newton's edition of *Paradise Lost*, 2 vols.
quarto. London, 1749. There are two varieties of this, one being without
the stone rectangular frame and without the date.

41. G. VERTUE, *sculpt.*
(**8**) Half length in oval, with slight scroll ornament above. Three-quarter
face to the right. Hair fairly long. Doublet buttoned down the front and
ornamented at the shoulders with lace ruff. Inscribed on a riband below
the oval:

Ioannes Milton
Ætatis Suæ. 21.

H. 6⅞. P.H. 3¾. W. 4½. P.W. 3¼.
Published in Newton's edition of *Paradise Regained*. 8vo. London, 1773.
Mentioned by Bromley.

42. J. HOUBRAKEN, *sculpt.* Amst. 1741.
(**9**) Half length in oval. Three-quarter face to the left. Hair fairly long.
Doublet buttoned down front and ornamented at shoulders, white lace
ruff. Stone frame to portrait inscribed "John Milton." Below is a book
with a lyre, a serpent with an apple in its mouth, a branch with leaves
and fruit and a roll of paper. Inscribed: "In the collection of the Right
Hon: Arthur Onslow Esqʳ Speaker of the House of Commons.
Impensis I. and P. Knapton, Londini, 174."
H. 15. P.H. 7. W. 9¾. P. W. 6¼.
One of the Series of folio plates known as Houbraken's heads.
Mentioned by Bromley.

43. 9a. Portrait similar to the last within a rectangle, on the top of which are
the words "Ms. Conv. Lex. No. 429," and below the rectangle "Stahlstich
von Karl Meyer in Nürnburg," and the name "Milton" within an engraved
tablet and above it the words "Inst. Bibl. Excudt."
H. 7. P.H. 4¾. W. 3½.

44. 9b. Lithograph portrait similar to the last, but rougher and coarser in
execution and inscribed: "Imp. litho de Melle Formentin rue St. André des
Arcs, No. 59." "J. Milton, Illustre Poëte Anglais."
H. 9. P.H. 7. W. 6.

ANDREW MILLER *fecit*. Dublin, 1744.
> **(10)** This is a copy of **(9)** in mezzotint, including the ornaments, but
> reversed and inscribed as above and also "Joannes Milton Ætatis XXI."
> On the pedestal is the motto "Nascuntur" etc.

Plate size 13½ by 10.

45. J. B. CIPRIANI, *engraver*.
> **(11)** Half length in oval. Three-quarter face to the right. Hair fairly long,
> doublet buttoned in front and ornamented at shoulders, white lace
> ruff. Oval is surrounded by a wreath of laurel. Below is the in-
> scription:

John Milton

Drawn and etched MDCCLX by J. B. Cipriani a Tvscan at the desire of
Thomas Hollis F.R. and A.S.S. from a pictvre in the collection of the Right Hon.
Arthur Onslow Speaker of the Commons Hovse Parliament.

> How soon hath Time the svttle theef of yooth
> Stoln on his wing my one and twentieth yeer
> My hasting dayes flie on with fvll career
> Bvt my late spring no bvd or blossom shew'th
> Perhaps my semblance might deceive the trvth
> That I to manhood am arriv'd so near
> And inward ripeness doth mvch less appear
> That som more timely-happy spirits indv'th
> Yet be it less or more or soon or slow
> It shall be still in strictest measvre eev'n

> To that same lot however mean or high
> Toward which time leads me and the will of heav'n
> All is if I have grace to vse it so
> As ever in my great Task Masters eye.

H. 10⅝. P.H. 6¼. W. 7. P.W. 4½.
> One of the Series mentioned in Hollis' *Memoirs*.

46. 11a. A proof of above plate, before letter.

47. ANON. *engraver.*
11b. Half length in oval. Three-quarter face to the right. Hair fairly long. Doublet with ornamentation at fastening and shoulders, white ruff. Inscribed above portrait John Milton. Under the portrait is written in ink "died 1674, aged 68."
H. 2⁵⁄₁₆. P.H. 2. W. 1⅞.

48. GOLDAR, *sculpt.*
(12) Half length in oval. Three-quarter face to the right. Hair fairly long. Doublet buttoned in front and ornamented at shoulders, white lace ruff. Oval medallion in rectangular frame, above which is inscribed:

> "London; Engrav'd for Harrison's Editions of Rapin.
> John Milton"

and below "In the Collection of the R^t Honble Arthur Onslow Esqr Published as the Act directs, May 28 1785."
H. 11⁵⁄₁₆. P. H. 6⁷⁄₁₆. W. 7⅞. P. W. 5⁷⁄₁₆.

49. ANON. *engraver.*
(13) Half length in oval. Three-quarter face to the left. Hair fairly long. Doublet buttoned down front and ornamented at shoulders, white lace ruff. Stone frame to portrait inscribed:

> John Milton.

Inscribed at the top "For the London Magazine" and at the foot "Publish'd by R. Baldwin at the Rose in Pater Noster Row 1752."
H. 7⅛. P.H. 3⅞. W. 4⅜. P.W. 3³⁄₁₆.
> For the *London Magazine*.

ANON. *engraver*.

(**14**) An oval representing masonry of six voussoirs, with segments cut off at top, bottom and sides. No plinth. "John Milton" at foot.

Plate size 4½ by 3½.

> This was issued in the fifth volume of the *British Biography* published by Baldwin, 7 vols., 8vo. London, 1766-72.

ANON. *engraver*.

(**15**) Oval in slightly ornamented frame, in the same plate with Algernon Sidney, John Hampden and Andrew Marvel, the frames being connected with interlacing ornament.

Size of each frame 2½ by 1¾.

I. JUNE, *sculpt*.

(**16**) Plain oval in same plate with Ben Jonson, Robert Boyle and John Locke.

2 by 1¾.

50. W. N. GARDINER, *sculpt*.

(**17**) Three-quarter face to the right. Long hair, white ruff, buttoned doublet. Inscribed:

> John Milton Ætat 21,
> From the original Picture in the Possession of
> Lord Onslow
> at Clandon in Surry.

purchased from the Executor of Milton's Widow by Arthur Onslow Esqʳ speaker of the House of Commons, as certified in his own hand writing at the back of the picture.

Publish'd June 4, 1794, by John and Josiah Boydell and George Nicol.
H. 10½. P.H. 6. W. 7⅜. P.W. 4¾.

> This appears in Boydell's *Milton*.

51. WOOLNOTH, *sculpt*.

(**18**) Inscribed: "John Milton Ætat XXI."

Marsh does not give any sizes for this plate. The portrait sizes are 3 × 2½.

ANON. *engraver*.

(**19**) Inscribed: Cornelius Jansen. W. C. Edwards. J. Yates, printer. London, John Macrone, St. James's Square, and E. Graves, King William St., Strand.

This, Marsh states, appeared in Macrone's edition, edited by Sir Egerton Brydges. No sizes are given and the picture is quite wrongly assigned to Cornelius Janssen.

52. CORNELIUS JANSEN. W. C. EDWARDS.

19a. Line engraving after the Onslow portrait, representing Milton at the age of twenty-one, with the usual white lace ruff and buttoned doublet. Beneath is a facsimile of the signature and date and below that the inscription:

Æt. XXI.

H. 7¼. W. 4⅜.

This is a vignette.

53, 54. EDWARD RADCLYFFE, *engraver*.

(**20**) Inscribed: "Milton aetat 21. After Vertue's engraving in 1731, from the original picture, then in the possession of the Right Hon. Speaker Onslow."

This appears in Masson's *Life of Milton*, in two different plates.

(A) P.H. 3½, P.W. 3. (B) A vignette P.H. 2, P.W. 2.

55. T. S. ENGLEHEART, *sc*.

19c. Inscribed "John Milton, aged 21. London, Published by John W. Parker, West Strand."

P.H. 3. P.W. 3.

MARSHALL'S ENGRAVING

W. MARSHALL, *sculpt*.

(**21**) This is the portrait which appeared in Humphrey Moseley's original edition of Milton's Poems in 1645, and has the celebrated Greek epigram beneath it. In the background is an arcadian scene, and in the four corners outside the oval the four muses, Melpomene, Erato,

Urania and Clio, with their names. The poet is within the oval, and has a lace bordered collar and lace bordered cuffs. The hair is long and there is a curtain at the back of the head. The inscription about the oval is: Ioannis Miltoni Angli Effigies Anno Ætatis viGess: Pri: Below the portrait is the Greek inscription in four lines, followed by the letters W. M. sculp.:

Ἀμαθεῖ γεγράφθαι χειρὶ τήνδε μὲν εικόνα
Φαίης τάχ᾽ ἂν, πρὸς εἶδος αὐτοφυὲς βλέπων.
Τὸν δ᾽ ἐκτυπωτὸν οὐκ ἐπιγνόντες, φίλοι
Γελᾶτε φαύλου δυσμίμημα ζωγράφου².

H. 6 ⁵⁄₁₆. P.H. 3⅝. W. 4 ³⁄₁₆. P.W. 2¹³⁄₁₆.
This print is exceedingly rare.

56. (22) There is an excellent copy of the same print in existence from the worn or possibly amended plate.

57. There is also a recent print from the second plate.

58, 59. M. V. DER GUCHT, *sculpt.*

(23) Half length in oval. Three-quarter face to the right. Long hair, buttoned coat, cloak over right shoulder, wide lace edged collar, flower stuck in coat just below collar, the left sleeve shows part of white undersleeve and wide lace edged cuff, the left hand and right arm and wrist being hidden by the cloak. Background a curtain looped back and showing a landscape with trees and three figures, one of whom is seated playing on a musical instrument, while the other two carry crooks and seem to be dancing. Round the oval is inscribed: "Ioannis Miltoni Angli Effigies. Anno Ætatis. 21." Below is inscribed: M. V. der Gucht sc. 1713. This is a reduced copy of the rare Marshall engraving and was prefixed to Tonson's Edition of *Paradise Regained*. 12mo. London, 1713.

---

² These lines have been roughly translated as follows:
Who, that my real lineament has scanned
Will not in this detect a bungler's hand?
My friends, in doubt on whom his art was tried,
The idiot limner's vain attempt deride.

H. 4¾. P.H. 3¼. W. 2¾. P.W. 2½.

This is in two states and printed in two different inks, one black the other brown.

Mentioned by Bromley.

FAITHORNE'S ENGRAVING

60. GUL. FAITHORNE ad Vivum Delin. et sculpsit.

(**24**) Three-quarter face to the right. Buttoned vest, gown, large white collar showing lace ends beneath, long hair. Oval, set on a pedestal on the top of which is engraved the name of the engraver, and on the front of it

Ioannis Miltoni Effigies Ætat: 62.
1670.

H. 8½. P. H. 4⅞. W. 6⅞. P. W. 4¼.

Published in Milton's *History of Britain*, 1670. Mentioned by Bromley. A rare print when in good condition.

61. (**25**) There is a modern copy of (**24**). The impressions are coarser.

62. 25a. There is also a recent print from the later plate which at one time belonged to Evans and is still in existence.

63. (**26**) A variety of (**24**), but the oval is represented as standing on a deep panelled surface, having in front Milton's arms and crest so as to form a folio plate.

8½ by 5¼.

This appeared in Toland's edition of "Milton's Prose Works," 1698. Each impression was struck from two plates, for which purpose the original had been cut away immediately below the name of the engraver, the oblique lines forming the ends of the upper surface of the pedestal erased, and the horizontal lines of heading continued to the edge of the plate. It is clear from the fact of these alterations that (**25**) was not struck from the original plate worn and retouched, but from a copy. The inscription reads "Ioannis Miltoni Effigies Natus Anno 1608 Obiit Anno 1674 Gul Faithorne ad vivum Belin et sculpsit."

64. FAITHORNE, *engraver.*

(**27**) Almost exactly the same as (**24**), but the plate has the appearance of having been cut down at the sides, and the engraver's name does not appear on the top of the pedestal. There is a similar inscription in the front of the pedestal, but the letters are smaller in size and closer together, and it is evident that the plate is not the same as that in (**24**), but a copy of it on a somewhat reduced scale.

H. 6⅝. P.H. 4⅜. W. 4¼. P.W. 3⅞.

65. 27a. No. **27** is known in two states in two different inks, the former very black, the latter greyish in tone.

W. DOLLE, *sculpsit.*

(**28**) This is a copy on a reduced scale from Faithorne's quarto and is inscribed "Ioannis Miltoni Effigies Aetat 63, 1671." It was published in *Artis Logicae plenior Institutio*, 12mo, London, 1672, and again in the second edition of *Paradise Lost* in 1674, and in the third edition in 1678.

Plate size 5 by 3.

ANON.

(**29**) A close copy of the last, except in features. Plate, a trifle smaller each way. Inscription and date same as (**28**).

66. I. SIMON, *fecit.*

(**30**) This is the very rare mezzotint in the British Museum. It is believed to be a portion of the plate described in Bromley's catalogue as a mezzotint, one of four portraits, the others being Beaumont, Fletcher and Cowley; but the ornamentation is different from these and other uniform portraits published by Bowles. Oval with a wavy fillet in the two upper corners. Marsh had only seen the one in the B. M. The Museum has now two impressions but the one in our collection is fully equal if not superior to the better of them. It is inscribed "Mr. John Milton obt anno 1674 ætat 66."

Size of plate 6¾ by 5.

67. R. WHITE, *sculpt.*

(**31**) Portrait in an oval frame of winged cherubs' heads and bold and peculiar scroll work, and at the foot in a rectangular tablet set in a richly ornamented frame Dryden's lines, here published for the first time.

H. 11. P.H. 5⅞. W. 7⅛. P.W. 4⅞.

This was issued in the fourth edition of *Paradise Lost*, folio, London, 1688, and in subsequent editions.

Mentioned by Bromley.

G. VERTUE, *sculp*.

(**32**) Portrait in an oval, sides partly concealed by a kind of architrave, top by a curtain looped up at the left by a fillet, terminated in a tassel on the right. On the curtain are the poet's name and date of death, "Ioannis Miltoni Effigies ob. 1674 Æt. 66," and in a framed panel at the foot within a peculiar scroll, Dryden's lines.

Size 8¾ by 6.

This appeared in Tonson's edition of the poetical works, two volumes, quarto, London, 1720. Mentioned by Bromley.

68. G. VERTUE, *sculp*.

(**33**) Half length in oval. Nearly full face, slightly to the left. Long hair, buttoned coat, cloak over left shoulder, white collar with lace ends of tie showing beneath. The oval is set in rectangular frame with curved top, which cuts the curve of oval at the sides. There is a curtain falling over the frame at the top and down the right side, ending with a tassel; on a curtain above the picture is inscribed:

"Ioannes Milton.
Ætatis LXII 1670."

Below is a tablet with leaf and scroll ornamentation inscribed:

Τὸν περὶ Μοῦσ' ἐφίλησε,
δίδου δ' ἀγαθόντε κακόντε·
Ὀφθαλμῶν μὲν ἄμερσε,
δίδου δ' ἡδεῖαν ἀοιδήν.
[*Odyssey*, Bk VIII. l. 63.]

Engraver's signature is on the lower corner of rectangular frame at the right.
H. 9⅛. P.H. 5⅛. W. 6⅜. P.W. 4⅝.

Published in Bentley's edition of Paradise Lost, 4to, London, 1732. Mentioned by Bromley.

69. G. VERTUE, *sculp*. 1747.

(**34**) Half length in oval. Nearly full face, slightly to the left. Long hair, buttoned coat, cloak over left shoulder, white collar with lace ends of tie showing beneath. The oval is set in rectangular frame with curved top, which cuts the curve of oval at the sides. There is a curtain falling over the frame at the top and down the right side, ending with a tassel; on the curtain above the picture is inscribed:

"Ioannes Milton.
Ætatis LXII 1670."

Below is a tablet with leaf and scroll ornamentation inscribed the same as on (**33**), being the quotation from the *Odyssey*, Bk VIII. l. 63. The engraver's signature is below the corner of rectangular frame at the right: below the left corner is inscribed "Front. Vol. 2."

H. 9⅛. P.H. 5⅛. W. 6⅜. P.W. 4⅜.

The same plate as preceding but with date altered.

Prefixed to the second volume of Newton's edition of *Paradise Lost*, 2 vols. 4to, London, 1749, which Hollis' Biographer inaccurately treats as the original condition of the plate.

J. GWIM, *sculpt*.

(**35**) This is a scarce print, evidently copied from Vertue's first quarto print after Faithorne. It is to be found in Grierson's edition of *Paradise Lost* and *Paradise Regained*, Dublin, 1724, but the book is a 12mo and the print has to be folded both ways to admit of its insertion.

70. G. VERTUE, *sculpt*.

(**36**) Half length, rectangular. Nearly full face, slightly to the right. Long hair, buttoned coat, cloak over right shoulder, white collar showing ends of tassels below. Inscribed:

Three Poets in three distant Ages born,
Greece Italy and England did adorn,
The First in loftiness of thought Surpas'd;

The Next in Majesty in both the Last.
The force of Nature cou'd no further goe:
To make a Third she joyn'd the former two.
                              DRYDEN.

H. 5. P.H. 3⅝. W. 3½. P.W. 2¾.
In the above "thought" is printed without a capital, "Surpas'd" with capital, and one "s" in last syllable, there is no comma after "majesty" and "former two" are in italics without capitals.

71. ANON. engraver.

(37) This is a similar portrait to the preceding one. Rectangular, with Dryden's lines and the name "Dryden" at the foot, and with the following peculiarities in the lines.

> "Thought" spelt with a capital.
> "surpass'd" with two s's at the end.
> Comma after Majesty.
> "Two" in Roman letters and with capital.

H. 4¾. P.H. 3¾. W. 3. P.W. 2⅝.
No name of engraver.

72. ANON. *engraver.*

(38) Half length, rectangular. Three-quarter face to the left. Long hair, buttoned coat, cloak over left shoulder, white collar showing lace ends of tie beneath. Inscribed:

> Three Poets in three distant Ages born
> Greece, Italy and England did adorn.
> The First in loftiness of thought Surpas'd;
> The Next in Majesty, in both the Last.
> The force of Nature cou'd no further goe;
> To make a Third she joyn'd the Former two.
>   DRYDEN.

H. 4¾. P.H. 3⅞. W. 2¾.
This is the edition in which the word "thought" is spelt without a capital. "Former" with a capital, there is a comma after Majesty, and no engraver's name.

73. FR. KYTE, *engraver*.

   38a. Mezzotint in laureated wreath with name on ribbon below.

   H. 11¾. P.H. 5¼. W. 9⅝. P.W. 4⅜.

      Published by Bowles in a set of four poets on one plate. See B. M.
   Burney, v. 37.

G. VERTUE, *sculpt*.

   (39) One of five ovals forming an 8vo page, the centre portrait being
   Chaucer and the others Milton, Butler, Cowley and Waller.

      One of the illustrations to Jacob's *Poetical Register*, 2 vols. 8vo,
   London, 1723.

74. ANON. *engraver*.

   (40) Portrait in Faithorne costume but with still further divergence in
   feature. In a circle formed by a serpent bordered at a distance of half an
   inch by a circular border extended at the sides by two shells and
   contracted at the top by the boundary of the plate, and at the bottom
   by a pedestal with the inscription:

      "Cui mens divinior, atque os
   Magna sonaturum."

Size of entire engraving, which has the appearance of a vignette, 3¾ by 2½.

ANON. *engraver*.

   (41) Portrait in a circle one inch in diameter, on a wreathed pedestal
   between two sphynxes in the attitude of heraldic supporters.

75. ANON. *engraver*.

   41a. Portrait in a circle on which is inscribed the word "Milton."

   H. 1½. P.H. 1½.

ANON. *engraver*.

   (42) In an oval on a diapered ground partly covered at foot by a border of
   acanthus leaves surrounding a vignette of the Temptation. At the
   corners formed by the lower part of the oval are several volumes, two
   open inscribed "Comus" and "Lycidas."

Plate 4¾ by 2¾.

Inscribed: "The Effigie of John Milton: author of Paradise Lost." The only copy of this seen by Mr. Marsh was the one in his own possession.

76. G. FAITHORNE, *del*. LANDON, *direx*.

(**43**) A copy of the Faithorne print in outline, in rectangular frame composed of four double lines and inscribed:

"Tome XXIX. Page 59.
Hist. D'Angleterre."

H. 5¼. P.H. 2⅝. W. 3¼. P.W. 2.

77. GUL. FAITHORNE, *ad viv. del.* CAR. KNIGHT, *sculpt.*

(**44**) Half length in oval. Three-quarter face to the right. Long hair, buttoned coat, cloak, white collar, ends of lace tie showing beneath collar. In oval frame resting on stone base which is inscribed:

"Joannis Miltoni
.Æt. LXII * MDCLXX.
Sana. Posteritas. Sciet."

H. 6¾. P.H. 4¼. W. 4¾. P.W. 3½.
This was prefixed to Capel Loftt's second edition of the first and second books of *Paradise Lost*, published at Bury St. Edmunds in 1793.

78. WILLIAM FAITHORNE, *engraver.*

(**45**) Oval with an outer line border. Inscribed "John Milton aged 62. Engraved from an Original by William Faithorne. Published 1670. Pubd. 13 June 1796 by I. & H. Richter, No. 26, Newman St., Oxford Road."
H. 12. P.H. 4¾. W. 9¾. P.W. 4.

79. FAITHORNE, *Pinx*. 1670. WOODMAN, Junr., *fc*.

(**46**) Half length rectangular. Three-quarter face to the right. Long hair, buttoned coat, cloak draped round shoulders and across breast, white collar with ends of white lace tie showing beneath it. Above the portrait is a trumpet with wreath of laurel leaves. Below is a line of scroll and leaf design and beneath that a sarcophagus engraved "Milton," with a garland of laurel leaves looped through its rings and with griffin feet; beside the casket are laurel leaves and the caduceus.

H. 6⅞. P. H. 3½. W. 4¼. P. W. 2¾.

Published Nov. 1, 1807 by Mathews and Leigh, intended for but not used
    in *The Cabinet or Monthly Report of Polite Literature*.

P. ROBERTS, *sculpt.*
   (**47**) No size is given of this print in Marsh's list. It is described as possessing
       no background and being published by T. Dolby, October 1, 1821.

80. H. ROBINSON, *sculpt.*
   (**48**) Oval finely engraved, having facsimile of autograph below the oval,
       and inscribed "London, William Pickering, 1831."
   H. 7½. P.H. 2¾. W. 4¾. P.W. 2¼.

81. COCHRAN, *sculpt.*
   (**49**) Portrait inscribed with facsimile of autograph, name of engraver, and
       "Gul. Faithorne ad Vivum del." No size given by Marsh. Inscribed
       "Engraved for Ivimey's *Life of Milton*. London, Published by
       Effingham Wilson, 88 Royal Exchange, Jany 5, 1833."

82. W. C. EDWARDS, *engraver.*
   (**50**) Half length, rectangular. Three-quarter face to the left. Long hair,
       buttoned coat, cloak over left shoulder, white collar. Inscribed:

"John Milton
Published by Westley and Davis, London."

   H. 10½. P.H. 5. W. 7. P.W. 4.
   This was prefixed to Fletcher's edition of the prose works, royal 8vo,
       London, 1833.
   This and the next two have a softened expression in the features.

83. W. C. EDWARDS, *engraver.*
   50a. Half length, rectangular. Three-quarter face to the left. Long hair,
       buttoned coat, cloak over left shoulder, white collar showing lace ends
       of tie. Inscribed:

"John Milton."

   H. 9½. P.H. 5. W. 7. P.W. 4.
   Without name of publisher. On rough paper.

84. 50b. Proof of above on India paper.

85. 50c. Softened portrait in a rectangle of horizontal lines enclosed in a line
border. Inscribed "Milton, London, Frederick Warne & Co."
H. 8. P.H. 2½. W. 5¼. P.W. 3.

86. ANON. *engraver.*
(**51**) Rectangular, portrait in an outline frame of scroll-work. Inscribed:

"Milton
London: L. Tallis."

H. 8¾. P. H. 4⅜. W. 5⅝. P. W. 3¼.
This was published in Leonard Townsend's *Alphabetical Chronology of
Remarkable Events.*

(**52**) Marsh describes a neatly finished octagonal modern engraving known
to him only as a proof before letters. 3½ by 3.

87. W. HUMPHREYS, *engraver.* From a Print by Faithorne.
(**53**) Three-quarter face to the right. Buttoned vest, gown, square white
collar showing cord and tassels, long hair. Rectangular. Inscribed with
a facsimile of Milton's signature and above it a facsimile of his
inscription in his copy of Aratus now in the British Museum, "Cum
sole, et Lunâ semper Aratus erit." Beneath the signature is the date
1631.
H. 8⅜. P.H. 4⅞. W. 5¼. P.W. 3⅞.
This was published by William Pickering of London, April 23, 1851, and
as a rule an inscription to that effect appears on the print.

88. HENRY COOK, *engraver.*
53a. In an oval with an exterior line border. Below the oval an engraved
tablet representing the serpent and lightning. Inscribed: "Milton,
London. Published as the Act directs April 15th, 1815, by G. Jones."
H. 9. P.H. 4½. H. of tablet 1. W. 5½. P.H. 3½. W. of tablet 1¾.

89. H. ADLARD, *sculpt.*
53b. Vignette portrait inscribed "Milton."
H. 4¾. P.H. 1½. W. 2¾. P.W. 1½.

90. H. ADLARD, *engraver*.

53c. Outline engraving in a rectangle of perpendicular lines with an exterior border of three lines, having below the rectangle a shield enclosing a single headed eagle and inscribed "John Milton," with also a facsimile of the signature. "Engraved by H. Adlard after the original Print by G. Vertue."

H. 7¾ P.H. 4½. W. 5. P.W. 3¾.

91. 53d. Proof on India paper of a reduction of (**53**).

ENGRAVINGS DERIVED FROM THE FAITHORNE PORTRAIT

92. J. B. CIPRIANI, *engraver*.

(**54**) Half length in oval. Nearly full face, slightly to the right. Long hair, buttoned coat, cloak, white collar, lace ends of tie showing beneath. The oval is surrounded by a wreath of laurel. Below is inscribed:

"Iohn Milton

Drawn and etched MDCCLX by I. B. Cipriani a Tvscan at the desire of Thomas Hollis F.R. and A.S.S. from a portrait in crayons now in the possession of Mess. Tonson Booksellers in the Strand London.

—— I sing with mortal voice vnchang'd
To hoarce or mvte thovgh fall'n on evil dayes
On evil dayes thovgh fall'n and evil tongves
In darkness and with dangers compast rovnd
And solitvde ——."

H. 10¾. P.H. 6½. W. 7. P.W. 4⅞.
This forms one of the Hollis series already alluded to.

93. J. HALL, *sculpt*.

(**55**) Portrait in an oval suspended from a wreath of ribbon, the name below on a tablet and the whole enclosed in a rectangle of engraved work. Inscribed: "Printed for John Bell, near Exeter Exchange London. Mar. 1st, 1777."

H. 5. P.H. 2. W. 3¼. P.W. 1⅝.

(**56**) There is another very similar to (**55**) appearing in Bell's *British Poets*.

94. MILTON, *sculpt.* From VERTUE.

(**57**) Inscribed above the poet's name:

"Publish'd by Harrison & Co. Decr. 1795."

H. 3¼. P.H. 1⅞. W. 2¾. P.W. 1⁷⁄₁₆.
This was engraved as a vignette illustration to a short biographical notice.

95. 57a. The print is also known, set within an octagon of wavy parallel horizontal lines.

96. J. MILLER, *sculpt.*

(**58**) Nearly full face. Buttoned vest, gown, square white collar showing tassels underneath, long hair. In an oval much covered with drapery, and beneath in a circle a lyre and laurel branches. The only inscription is the name of the engraver.
H. 5½. P.H. 3¼. W. 3¼. P.W. 2¾.

HOLBROOK, *sculpt.*

(**59**) This is a bad copy of (**58**), reversed, and with Dryden's lines at the foot. It is prefixed to some copies of the prose retranslation of *Paradise Lost*, from Raymond de St. Maur, 8vo, London, 1773.

N. PARR, *sculpt.*

(**60**) An oval, 1½ by 1, suspended by a ribbon. Inscribed "I. Milton." There is an example of this in the Tangye collection.

97. BARTOLOZZI, *sculpt.*

(**61**) A circle partly surrounded by laurel branches and fillet, on a pedestal inscribed "Milton."
4¾ by 2¾.

98. R. H. CROMEK, *sculp.*

(**62**) Very similar to the last. Inscribed "Milton" on a panel.
3¾ by 2½.

HEATH, *sculpt.*

(**63**) Resembling (**62**). Inscribed: "From an original painting." Published in Aikin's *British Poets*, 1802.

W. T. FRY, *engraver*.

(64) Ornamented rectangular frame, inscribed "Milton" on a festoon overhanging the top. "Published by Thomas Tegg." This appears in Howard's *Beauties of Milton*.

ANON. *engraver*.

(65) One of three portraits in circles, 1¼ in diameter, in the title-page of the *Beauties of Milton, Thomson and Young*. Published by Kearsley. 12mo, London, 1783.

A. HAENISH, *delt*.

(66) A folio print or lithograph (?), inscribed: "John Milton. Schenck & MacFarlane, Lithographers, Edinburgh." Marsh does not give the size.

The White Portrait or Simon's Folio Mezzotint

99. R. WHITE, *ad Vivum delin*. J. SIMON, *fecit*.

(67) Mezzotint. Oval, in a frame work of imitation stone, only the four corners of the frame work being visible. Three-quarter face to the left. Buttoned vest, gown, white collar showing cord and tassels, long hair, laurel wreath as in the Richardson etching. Inscribed:

"Mr. John Milton"

with Dryden's lines in double columns, and following them: "Sold by T. Bowles in Pauls Church Y^d & I. Bowles in Cornhill."

H. 13¼. P.H. 11¼. W. 9½. P.H. 9⅛.

 Mentioned by Bromley.

 Mentioned in the Sutherland Collection.

 Exceedingly rare.

There are two states of this, we exhibit both.

100. I. C. BOOK, *fc*.

67a. In an oval surrounded by an outer border of engraved work. Inscribed "Milton."

H. 7. P.H. 4¼. W. 4½. P.W. 3½.

101. (68) A composition containing in the foreground a bust of Milton copied from (67), and in the background pictures of Cowley and Denham, the

three names inscribed on a panel at foot. Inscribed: "Engraved by Anthony Cardon from a drawing by Thomas Uwius after the original of Sir Peter Lely and R. White, and Published 1 November, 1805 by John Sharpe."

102. 68a. A variety of the above does not give the name of the engravers or the publishers, nor the statement respecting the original painters, but only the three names on the panel.

(69) Marsh describes an oval, 2½ by 2¼, known to him only as a proof before letters. The portrait is without the wreath which appears in **(67)**, but the print has clearly been copied, he says, from Simon's rather than from Richardson's portrait.

WHITE-RICHARDSON LIKENESSES

103. ANON. *etcher.*
(70) Three-quarter face to the right. Buttoned vest, gown, white collar, long hair, laurel wreath surrounding head. Inscribed:

"J.R. sen. f. From an Excel^t. Orig. (Crayons) in his Collection,"
"Nectens aut Paphia Myrti, aut Parnasside Lauri
Fronde comas, at ego secura pace quiescam.
MILTON'S *Mansus.*"

H. 6. W. 4.
The laurel branch on the right temple consists of eleven leaves.
Mentioned by Bromley.

104. ANON. *etcher*, but almost certainly Richardson.
(71) Etching almost exactly resembling **(70)**, and lettered as it, but slightly smaller in size, the drapery continued a little lower down on the chest, and the laurel branch on the right temple consisting of nine leaves instead of eleven.

H. 6⅛. W. 3½.

G. BARRON, *delt et fecit.*
(72) An etching inscribed Milton, copied from Richardson's original but reversed. Size not given.

105. ANON. *engraver.*

(**73**) An engraving reduced from Richardson's etching, but reversed as in
the last. Size, exclusive of lettering, which is copied from Richardson,
4 by 2¾.

106. J. RICHARDSON, *f.*

(**74**) Half length, rectangular. Nearly full face, slightly to the right, no
laurel wreath. Long hair, buttoned coat, gown, white collar showing
loops of cord and tassels at throat. Inscribed:

> "Authentic Homer Light's whole Fountain flows,
> Immense! Feirce Dazling yet, & Torrent Glows:
> His Temper'd Beam the Mantuan Bard reflects,
> Shines Sweeter, & his Fairest Rays Selects:
> Thine Milton Both, but not Both These Alone,
> Thou, Like Elysium, Know'st Another Sun."
>
> J. R. jun.

H. 8⅛. W. 5¾.

It is probable that only the verses are by the younger Richardson.

107. 74a. There are two states of this, the above being printed in black ink and
74a in brown, the latter is the rarer and is generally foxed.

ANON. *etcher.*

(**75**) An etching in Richardson's manner without lettering, but on a larger
scale and with a somewhat different expression. Size 9¾ by 7½.

J. ROPER, *engraver.*

(**76**) Oval, 2½ by 2. This forms a vignette in the engraved title of Parson's
edition of *Paradise Lost*, royal 8vo, London, 1796.

WHITE-VERTUE LIKENESSES, OR VERTUE (1725)

108. GEO. VERTUE, *sculp.* 1725.

(**77**) Three-quarter face to the right. Cloak, buttoned vest, white collar
showing tassels, long hair. In an oval composed of ornamental masonry,
the age and date "Ioannes Milton Ætat: 62. A.D. 1670" upon the frame
and on a block above. At the foot of the oval in an escutcheon is a single

headed eagle intended to represent Milton's arms, and below on a panelled block Dryden's lines "Three poets," etc. Inscribed:

"Illustrissimo D^{no} D^{no} Algernon Comiti de Hertford D^{no} Percy &c. &c. Obsequentissime D.D.D.

G. VERTUE."

H. 14½. P.H. 8. W. 9⅜. P.W. 7⅛.
Mentioned by Bromley.

109. OWEN, *engraver.*

(**78**) Portrait in an oval set within a white border and having a tablet below with the name, the whole set within a rectangle of horizontal lines, surrounded by a single line border. Inscribed "John Milton Ætat. 62" within the tablet, and below the rectangle "Engraved by Owen, from a drawing by Vertue, in the Collection of Thos. Brand Hollis Esq. Published by R. Wilks, 89, Chancery Lane."

H. 8¼. H. of rectangle 6¼. P.H. 3½. H. of tablet 1⅛. W. 5½. W. of rectangle 3¾. P.W. 2¾. W. of tablet 2¾.

110. VERTUE, *delin^t.* W. N. GARDINER, *sculpt.*

(**79**) Three-quarter face to the left. Long hair, buttoned vest, gown, white collar showing tassels. Inscribed:

"Iohn Milton Ætat 62.
From the Original Drawing by Vertue in the Collection of Thos. Brand Hollis Esqr. at the Hyde Essex. Published, June 4, 1794, by Iohn & Josiah Boydell & Geo. Nicol."

H. 10⅜. P.H. 6. W. 7¼. P.W. 4¾.

This forms one of the series of three portraits in Boydell's *Milton*, the other two being the Janssen and Onslow portraits.

N.B. The original drawing by Vertue for this engraving is in Dr. Williamson's collection. It was originally at Strawberry Hill.

111. BLOOD, *sc.*

(**80**) Rectangular, in a plain line frame having the name on a tablet beneath, and inscribed "John Milton. Published by Longman, Hurst, Rees & Orme, Paternoster Row, 1809." H. 6½. P.H. 3½. W. 4½. P.W. 2¾.

112. 80a. A proof is known without the tablet and name and without the imprint.

113. R. COOPER, *engraver.*

(**81**) Half length, rectangular. Nearly full face, slightly to the right. Long hair, buttoned coat, cloak over right shoulder, white collar showing loops of cord and tassels at throat. Inscribed:

"Milton

Engraven from an original Picture, for the 7th being the supplemental Number to the New Series of La Belle Assemblée. Published July 1, 1810, by J. Bell, Southampton Street, Strand, London."

H. 9⅛. P.H. 3⅞. W. 5½. P.W. 3¼.

114. ANON. *engraver.*

(**82**) Half length, rectangular. Three-quarter face to the right. Long hair, buttoned coat, cloak over right shoulder, white collar showing loops of cord and tassels at throat. Inscribed, facsimile of autograph, "John Milton (1667)." "Published by William Pickering, Chancery Lane, 1826."

H. 8⅝. P.H. 2⁹⁄₁₆. W. 5⅝. P.W. 2.

Prefixed to Pickering's three vol. edition of the Poetical Works, 1667.

115. R. HICKS, *sculpt.*

(**83**) Portrait in a rectangle. Inscribed "William Faithorne del. R. Hicks sculp. London. Published by Thomas Kelly, Paternoster Row, June 1, 1829." With facsimile of autograph.

H. 8½. P.H. 3. W. 5¼. P.W. 2½.

116. R. HICKS, *engraver.* From a Painting by W. Faithorne.

83a. Three-quarter face to the right. Buttoned vest, gown, square white collar showing cord and tassels, long hair. Rectangular, in an ornamental stone frame surrounded by curtains and having on one side a painter's palette with brushes, compasses, rule and hammer, and on the other the Bible with chalice and paten, while above is a symbolical group comprising two seated figures, one drawing and the other reading, and between them a bust of Pallas, with a globe, mask, lyre, scroll and wreath, the whole illuminated by the rays of the sun. Below the portrait are the words John Milton on the stone pedestal, and below again a facsimile of the poet's signature with the statement as to the engraver and the following words:

"London: Published by Thomas Kelly, 17, Paternoster Row, 1830."

H. 10. P.H. 3⅛. W. 6⅜. P.W. 2⅜.

The above differs slightly from No. **83**. The date is a year later and the inscription not quite the same.

117. **83**b. The same as 83a, but without the ornamental frame and without any lettering whatever. Proof on India paper.

118. VERTUE. W. C. EDWARDS.

(**84**) Three-quarter face, turned to the left. White collar, gown, long hair. Facsimile of autograph beneath portrait. Inscribed:

"London, John Macrone, 3, Sᵗ James's Square, 1835."

H. 8. P.H. 4. W. 6. P.W. 3⅜.

This was published in the six volume edition of the Poetical Works edited by Sir Egerton Brydges. The list of illustrations erroneously describes it as a portrait of Milton in his sixty-second year, from an original portrait of Faithorne's drawing.

ANON. *engraver.*

(**85**) Rectangular, 1½ by 1. In a frame of outline scroll work. Inscribed "John Milton."

119. E. G. SCHMIDT, *sculpsit.*

(**86**) Portrait in an oval of stone work resting upon a pedestal. Between portrait and pedestal is an escutcheon with a single headed eagle intended to represent Milton's arms. Inscribed: "Jean Milton. Né à Londres en 1608. Mort en 1674. Agé de 66 ans. A Paris chez Odieuvre Mᵈ d'Estampes, Quay de l'Ecole, vis-àvis la Samarit. a la belle Image, C.P.R."

H. 5¾. P.H. 3½. W. 4¼. P.W. 3.

120. ANON.

(**87**) Portrait within an oval set in masonry, having the name and style on a scroll and the name of the publisher and the lines of verse on a pedestal below. The portrait is three-quarter face to the right. Buttoned vest, gown, white collar showing tassels. Inscribed:

"Jean Milton,
Auteur du Poëme du Paradis perdu et de celui du Paradis retrouvé né à Londres en 1608, mort en 1674. Suite de Desrochers. Se vend Paris chez Petit à la Couronne d'épines rue S. Iacques."
Par la sublimité de son double Poëme,
Le célèbre Milton semble être Homere meme;
Et si ces grands auteurs sont fort pareils entre eux,
Par leur esprit fécond et rempli de lumières,
La malice du sort offusquant leurs paupières,
Pour mieux les rendre égaux, les aveugla tous deux.

H. 6⅛. P.H. 3⅞. W. 4¼. P.W. 3¼.

121. 87a. A variety of this has a different publisher's name, and is inscribed:

"à Paris, chés (*sic*) Daumont rue St. Martin."

F. BONNEVILLE, *del.*

(**88**) Oval 4 by 3½. Inscribed "J. Milton. Né à Londres le 9 Xbre 1608. Mort à Brunhill (Bunhill Fields) le 15 Nbre 1674."

WHITE-VAN DER GUCHT ENGRAVING

122. JNO VANDER GUCHT, *sculp.*

(**89**) Portrait in an oval of stone work on which is inscribed the name of the engraver and "Giovanni Milton." At the foot of the oval is an escutcheon with a single headed eagle, helmet, crest, mantling and various ornaments, terms, harps, wreaths and stars.

H. 12¼. P.H. 7¾. W. 8¼. P.W. 6½.

In the Italian translation of *Paradise Lost* by Paolo Rolli, folio, London, 1736.

MOLLISON, *sculpt.*

> **89**a. There is a vignette from the same portrait inscribed "John Milton, Mollison sculpt." An example of it is in the B.M.

123. N. PARR. *sculp.*

> **(90)** An oval with somewhat similar ornaments. Inscribed "Joannes Milton."

Size of engraving 5¾ by 3⅜.

There is a fine example of this rare print in the Tangye collection.

ANTONIO BARATTI, *sculpt.*

> **(91)** Oval on a pedestal. Inscribed "Giovanni Milton."

Plate size 5 by 2¾.

Issued in the edition of Rolli's translation, 12mo, Paris, 1758.

THE BAKER DRAWING, ETC.

124. J. MILLER, *sc.*

> **(92)** Half length in oval. Nearly full face, slightly turned to the left. Long hair, buttoned coat, cloak, white collar. Portrait is in wooden surrounded by a fringed drapery. Below is an engraving of the angel driving Adam and Eve from the garden, partially concealed by the drapery, in the folds of which are a lyre and laurel leaves.

H. 7. P.H. 3⅜. W. 4⁹⁄₁₆. P.W. 2⅞.

This was prefixed to the edition of *Paradise Lost* edited by Newton, printed by Baskerville and published by J. and R. Tonson, 4to, Birmingham, 1759.

125. ANON. *engraver.*

> **(93)** As **(92)** but smaller part of the frame at the top and draperies at the base and sides being cut away. There is no engraver's name.

H. 6⅜. P.H. 3⅜. W. 4. P.H. 2⅞.

This was the same as **(92)** but cut down to adapt it to an 8vo volume and prefixed to Newton's *Paradise Lost*, 8th edit., 2 vols. 8vo, London, 1778.

J. BAKER, *sculpt.*

> (**94**) Inscribed "John Milton. Born 1608. Died 1674. T. Simpson delin. J. Baker sculp. From the original drawing by Faithorne in the possession of William Baker Esq."
>
> Size 4¾ by 3¾.
>
> Prefixed to the first edition of Todd's *Milton*, six volumes, 8vo, London, 1801.

126. T. COLLYER, *engraver.*

> (**95**) Inscribed "John Milton. Born 1608. Died 1674. From the original Painting by Faithorne in the possession of William Baker Esqr. Drawn by T. Simpson. Published 1809, by F. C. & J. Rivington, St. Pauls Church Yard."
>
> Sizes as (**94**).
>
> Published in the second edition of Todd's *Milton*, 1809.

T. A. DEAN, *engraver.*

> (**96**) Similar to (**95**) and with similar inscription save as to the engraver's name.
>
> Size 4¾ by 3¾.
>
> Published in the third edition of Todd's *Milton*, 1826. A variety of this plate was prefixed to the fourth edition in 1851 lettered "John Milton, Faithorne pinxit. Dean sculpt."

> (**97**) A neat copy of (**96**). Inscribed "Faithorne pinxt. Dean sculp. Published by J. G. & F. Rivington, 1833." Was prefixed to an edition of *Paradise Lost* issued by the S.P.C.
>
> Size 3½ by 3, exclusive of lettering.

127. HOLL, *engraver.*

> (**98**) Half length in oval. Three-quarter face to the right. Long hair, buttoned coat, cloak over right shoulder, white collar showing loops of cord and tassels at throat. Inscribed:
>
> "John Milton Ætat 62.
London: Published Nov. 23d 1799, by T. Heptinstall Holborn."
>
> H. 7⅞. P.H. 4¼. W. 5¾. P.W. 3¼.

128. 98a. There is a variety of above, with a different imprint, reading "Printed for Verner & Hood & the other Partners."

129. HOLL, *engraver.*
98b. Small portrait in oval by Holl, with biography of Milton in forty-six lines below it. H. 3. P.H. 1⅞. W. 6. P.W. 1½.

J. ARCHER, *engraver.*
(**99**) A close copy of (**98**). Inscribed "John Milton." "Engraved by J. Archer for the select Portrait Gallery in the Guide to Knowledge."

W. FRENCH, *sc.*
(**100**) A copy of the same print in a border of irregular form of curtains and wreaths, 6 inches in diameter, forms a plate in Wright's *Universal Pronouncing Dictionary*, royal 8vo. No date. It is inscribed "Milton. W. French sc. John Tallis & Co., London and New York."

130. W. FRENCH, *sc.*
100a. Engraving in florid ornamental frame with laurel wreaths and tassels. Inscribed:

"Milton

London: E. T. Brain & Co. 88, Fleet Street."

H. 9¼. P.H. 4¾. W. 7⅝. P.W. 3⅞.

131. 100b. A variety is inscribed:

"Verlag der Englischen Kunstanstalt von A. H. Payne in Leipzig."

(**101**) A copy from (**100**) rather coarsely executed in the chalk manner of engraving, with lyre and laurel wreath lightly sketched in behind the head.
Size of plate 4¾ by 3.
Appears in Darton's *Cabinet of Portraits*, vol. I. Inscribed "John Milton," with five lines of biographical notice engraved. London, Darton, 1822.

(**102**) A copy of (**101**) in a suspended frame with ornamented corners at the bottom of which is inscribed "Milton."
Outside size 3 by 2¾.

132. MARIANO BOVI, *engraver.*

(**103**) Half length in oval. Three-quarter face to the right. Long hair, buttoned coat, cloak, white collar with tassels showing below. Inscribed:

"Giovanni Milton.
Onorate L'altissimo Poeta."
"Engraved by Mariano Bovi."

H. 7⅞. P.H. 5⅝. W. 4¹³⁄₁₆. P.W. 4¼.

(**104**) A similar plate to (**103**). Inscribed "Giovanni Milton. Nato li 9 Xbre 1608. Morto li 15 9bre 1674. B. Musitelli inc." It is prefixed to Scolari's *Saggio di Critica sul Paradiso Perduto*, quarto, Venezia, 1818.

VERTUE'S ENGRAVING (1750)

133. G. VERTUE, 1750.

(**105**) Half length in oval. Three-quarter face to the right. Long hair, buttoned coat, cloak, white collar with lace ends of tie showing beneath. Set in oval medallion with ribbon and shell ornament at the top inscribed "Milton." The medallion stands on a pedestal with leaf decoration at the corners. H. 6½. P.H. 3⅞. W. 4⅜. P.W. 3³⁄₁₆.

Published in Newton's edition of *Paradise Lost.* 2 vols. 8vo, London, 1750, and again in 1778.

134. G. VERTUE (the G and V blended in monogram), *sc.*

(**106**) Half length. Nearly full face, slightly turned to the right. Long hair. Gown over buttoned coat. White collar, tassels showing beneath. Upper corners rectangular, bottom curved showing frame. Below is a tablet inscribed "John Milton."

H. 5½. P.H. 3¾. W. 3¼. P.W. 2⅝.

From Tonson's edition of *Paradise Lost*, 12mo, London, 1751.

135. G. V. *sc.* 1756.

(**107**) Size and arrangements exactly as the preceding one, but the features still more unsatisfactory.

This appeared in one of the 12mo editions of *Paradise Lost* published with Fenton's *Life.*

135a. G. FRITZSCH, *sculps.* 1761.

Similar portrait to the last, but in an oval of stone work, and mounted on a plinth of the same, inscribed: "Milton." This appears in a German translation of *Paradise Lost*. Altona, 1762. 8vo.

Ornamented and engraved by J. CHAPMAN, 1804.

(**108**) A portrait evidently copied from (107). Inscribed "John Milton." "Ornamented and Engraved by J. Chapman, 1804. Published by James Cundee." It is an octagon, 2½ by 1¾, surmounted by a dove and with a serpent, cross and ornament at the foot.

Prefixed to Evans' edition of *Paradise Lost*, in 2 vols., small 8vo.

CHAPMAN, *sc.*

(**109**) A more pleasing version of the same portrait forms the vignette to the engraved title of a small edition of the poetical works published by Suttaby, 1805. It is an oval. Inscribed: "Milton. Engraved by Chapman."

Size 1¾ by 1¼.

There is an example in the B.M. inscribed: "Published Oct. 31, 1800, by George Nicholson, Poughmill near Ludlow. Sold in London by T. Carden, Bucklersbury: Champante and Whitrow, 4 Jewry Street, Aldgate: R. Bickerstaff, 210 Strand: and by all other booksellers.

PORTRAITS DERIVED FROM BUSTS, MEDALLIONS, SEALS, ETC.

FROM THE BUST BELONGING TO MR. HOLLIS

136. I. RICHARDSON, *delin.* G. VERTUE, *sculpsit.*

(**110**) A bust on a pedestal decorated with a serpent and an apple and with the poet's name inscribed on the plinth. The bust stands in a round headed niche of masonry.

H. 12¾. S.H. 12. W. 7¾. S.W. 7.

This appeared in the edition of Milton's prose works, 2 vols. folio, London, 1738.

The impression in the B.M. has a long MS. note on it in handwriting believed to be that of Thos. Brand Hollis.

G. VERTUE, *sculpsit*.

(**111**) Identical with (**110**) but cut down a little above the spring of the circular head of the niche so as to reduce the size to 10 by 7. Issued in Baron's edition of the Prose Works, 2 vols. quarto, London, 1753.

E. VERHELST, *fec*.

(**112**) A small bust evidently intended for a copy of the preceding. Inscribed: "Milton. E. Verhelst fec. Mannheim."

137. I. B. CIPRIANI, *engraver*.

(**113**) Half length in oval. Three-quarter face to the right. Long hair, buttoned coat, white collar. The oval is surrounded by a wreath of leaves with entwined ribbon. Inscribed:

"Iohn Milton
Drawn and etched MDCCLX by I. B. Cipriani a Tvscan from a bvst in plaister modelled from the life now in the possession of Thomas Hollis F.R. and A.S.S."

> Cyriac this three years day these eyes thovgh clear
> To ovtward view of blemish or of spot
> Bereft of light their seeing have forgot
> Nor to their idle orbs doth sight appear
> Of svn or moon or star throvghovt the year
> Or man or woman yet I argve not
> Against Heav'n's hand or will not bate one iot
> Of heart or hope bvt still bear vp and steer
> Right onward What svpports me dost thov ask
> The conscience friend to have lost them over-ply'd
> In liberties defence my noble task
> Of which all Evrope rings from side to side
> This thovght might lead me throvgh this world's vain mask
> Content thovgh blind had I no other gvide.

H. 10¾. P.H. 6¼. W. 7⅛. P.W. 4½.

One of the Hollis plates already alluded to.

138. H. MEYER.

(**114**) Bust. Profile to the left. Long hair, buttoned coat, wide collar. Inscribed:

"John Milton,
Engraved by H. Meyer, from a Drawing by Mr. Cipriani, in the
Possession of the Rev. Dr. Disney. Published April 16, 1810, by T. Cadell &
W. Davies, Strand, London."

H. 9. S.H. 8½. W. 6. S.W. 5½.

On India paper. There is a proof before letters in the B. M.

139. 114a. A variety of this is lithographed on plain white paper, and is
slightly different in the shading of the background.

(**115**) A representation of the same bust appears in the *Literary Magazine,*
and on the inscription Literary is spelt with two "t" 's.

Size, exclusive of lettering, 2½ by 2¾.

(**116**) The same appears with the title of the periodical spelled correctly.

RICHARDSON'S ETCHING

140. J. RICHARDSON, *f.*
(**117**) Bust. Three-quarter face to the right. Long hair, laurel wreath on
head, buttoned coat, cloak round shoulders, white collar, cord tied in a
bow with tassels at the throat. On the base of the bust are the letters
MIΛΤΩ. Below is the inscription:

> Forsitan & Nostros ducat de Marmorc Vultus,
> Nectens aut Paphia Myrti, aut Parnasside Lauri
> Fronde Comas, at ego Secura Pace Quiescam.
> MILTON in Manso.

H. 9⅜. W. 5¾.

141. 117a. The same as (**117**) but without inscription.

CLARK, *sculpt.*
(**118**) A small vignette is known enclosed in an abundance of foliated
ornament, a bad copy of the preceding. "Milton" is inscribed on the
pedestal.

77

142. J. RICHARDSON, 1738.

(**119**) Head in oval. Profile to the right. Long hair with band of ribbon round the head. Within the oval at the foot is inscribed "MIΛTΩ."

H. 5¾. P.H. 3⅞. W. 4⅛. P.W. 3½.
Mentioned by Bromley.

ANON. engraver.

(**120**) There is a profile in oval strongly resembling the preceding, but clothed and with a collar. In the style of the White-Richardson drawing.

F. P.

(**121**) There is a profile etching, a copy of (**120**), but reversed. Engraved by F. P., who Granger says, was Francis Perry, a pupil of Richardson.

MILTON VICTORIOUS OVER SALMASIUS

143. ANON. *engraver,* but almost certainly Cipriani.

(**122**) A quarto plate representing a terminal bust of Milton. On the face of the term is a volume lettered "Def. Pro Pop. Anglic."; and beneath a palm branch from which is suspended a medallion representing Salmasius. Inscribed: "I. B. C. I. F. MDCCLXVII. Life of M[*ilton*]. By I. T. Ed. II. P. LXXX."

H. 10. P.H. 2¾. W. 7½. P.W. 2½.

J. HOPWOOD, *sculpt.*

(**123**) There is a reduced copy of (**122**), 4½ by 3¼, the volume and palm branch superseded by a fillet inscribed with the words "Defensio secunda." The name of the engraver appears in lieu of the inscription, "Life of Milton," etc. Prefixed to the third volume of the works of Archdeacon Wrangham, 8vo, London, 1816.

(**124**) There is another variety of the same plate altered by the erasure of the fillet and portrait from the face of the term and substitution of the poet's name, "John Milton," and beneath, the words, "Do fermented liquors contribute to intellectual excellence."

NATHL. PARR, *sculpt.*

(**125**) Folio print, having the name "Milton" inscribed on the pedestal of a bust, and "H. Gravelot delin," while below on a panel is the following inscription:

> In the year of our Lord Christ one thousand seven hundred and thirty seven. This Bust of the Author of Paradice Lost was placed here by William Benson Esquire one of ye two Auditors of the Impress to His Majesty King George the Second formerly Surveyor General of the Works to His Majesty King George the First. Rysbrach was the Statuary who cut it.

Folio, 12 by 7½.

144. THORNTON, *engraver.*

(**126**) A reduced copy of the above is in 8vo. Inscribed: "The monument of the celebrated John Milton as it now stands in Westminster Abbey. Drawn by Hamilton, Engraved by Thornton."

There are certain changes in the inscription on the Monument in this print. Paradise is spelt with its correct s; Impress reads Impressts; ye reads the; Esquire reads Esqr.; and Rysbrach, Rysbrack.

145. 126a. There is a variety, inscribed "Le Bouit Delineavit et sculpsit ab Origine apud Westmonasterium Ecclesiam 1751." This was unknown to Marsh.

(**127**) A print is referred to by Granger and Bromley inscribed: "Johannes Miltonus M. Rysbrachius marm. sc. pro. Gul. Bensono arm. G. Vandergucht, 1741." Mr. Marsh had never seen it.

MISCELLANEOUS BUSTS

146. W. RIDLEY, *engraver.*

(**128**) In Cooke's edition of select poets appears a plate inscribed as follows: "Engraved by W. Ridley from a drawing taken from a bust in the possession of the proprietor. Printed for C. Cooke, 17, Paternoster Row, Jan. 7, 1800." Mr. Marsh knew nothing of the bust in question.

ANON. *engraver.*

(**129**) A miniature bust somewhat resembling the preceding.

ABR. RAIMBACH, *sculpt.*

(**130**) A frontispiece to Cowper's *Milton* represents a terminal bust, differing from all other likenesses, standing on a circular pedestal against which is a medallion of Cowper. It is inscribed: "Milton. Richd. Smirke delt. Abr. Raimbach sculpt. Published by Johnson & Co., 1810."

MEDALLIONS

147. J. HULETT, *del. et sculp.*

(**131**) A quarto plate in Peck's *Milton* represents the obverse and reverse of a medallion. Obverse inscribed: "Iohannes Miltonus. Tanner f." Reverse inscribed: "E. Marmore in Ecclesia Sancti Petri Apud Westmonasterium erectore Gulielmo Bensono arm. Anno salutis Humanae MDCCXXXVII Rysbrachius sculpsit." In a tablet between is ÆRE. ARG. AVRO. Beneath is the quotation from the *Odyssey:* "Τὸν πέρι Μοῦσ' ἐφίλησε" & c., and the dedication: "Viro ornatissimo Gulielmo Bensono Arm. Miltoni sui Tabulam hanc merito votivam D.D.D. Francüs Peck A.M."
H. 6¾. P.H. 2. W. 5½. P.W. 2.

J. WOOD, *sculpt.*

(**132**) A profile forming a medallion vignette, 2 inches in diameter, appears in the title-page of Dobson's Latin translation of the *Paradise Lost*, 2 vols., quarto, London, 1753. It is inscribed: "Joannes Miltonus. Guls. Green Jun. *delin*. J. Wood *sculp*."

(**133**) An engraving in outline from a medal has on the obverse a head apparently designed after the type of the White portrait, and inscribed: "Ioannes Milton." The reverse has the Temptation, partly surrounded by a fillet inscribed: "Dira dulce canit alter Homerus," and the initials "J. D."

148. A. SMITH, A.R.A., *sc.*

(**134**) Half length in oval. Profile to the right. Gown, white collar with tassels. Long hair. A medallion.

80

H. 6⅜. S.H. 2. W. 3⅞. S.W. 1¾.

This forms a vignette in the title-page to an edition of *Paradise Lost* published in 12mo by Sharp, 1809.

CHARLES HEATH, *sculpt.*

(**135**) A medallion in profile, inscribed: "John Milton. Charles Heath sculp. Published by J. Mawman, etc., 1817."

(**136**) There are ten medallion heads representing English poets ranged on the side of a representation of Mount Parnassus, in a folio print. They are inscribed: "R. Smirke *del*. J. Newton & J. Landseer *fecit*. Medallions per J. Newton." The head of Milton is copied from the Faithorne portrait.

SEALS

149. W. W. RYLANDS, *sculpt.*

(**137**) Profile portrait showing three buttons of the vest and part of the collar. Long hair. Inscribed: "Milton." "From a Drawing of Mr. Deacon, taken from an Impression of a Seal of T. Simon in the Possession of Mr. Yeo." Above the inscription is a small engraved oval intended to show the size of the seal. India paper. Mentioned by Bromley. The seal is referred to in Hollis's *Memoirs*. Very rare.

H. 4¼. P.H. 2⅛. H. of Seal ¾. W. 2¾. P.W. 1⅞. W. of Seal ⅝.

(**138**) In a worn plate appearing in an edition of Milton's works published by J. Smith, High Holborn, 1830, appears a print inscribed: "Milton." "From an impression of a seal of T. Simon in the possession of Mr. Yeo." A close inspection detects traces of the words "Engraved by" beneath the oval to the left, and a name to the right which Mr. Marsh was unable to decipher.

T. HOLLOWAY, *sculpt.*

(**139**) A similar print is inscribed: "Milton." "From an impression of a seal of T. Simon in the possession of Mr. Yeo. Published August 15, 1801, by J. Mawman, etc."

R. B. ROMNERY, *sculpt.*

(140) A rare and possibly unpublished print is a close and well executed copy of the preceding, having engraver's name as given.

N.B. There is a wax impression in the N. P. G. from a seal bearing the bust of Milton, but it is not known where the original seal or signet is.

Mr. Albert Way had a silver seal with Milton's arms on it, and a steel puncheon with a bust portrait, but neither item can be found.

PRETENDED PORTRAITS

THE COOPER MINIATURE

150. CAROLINE WATSON, *engraver.*

(141) Miniature portrait. Black gown with facings of velvet, white collar, long curly hair. Standing against a pyramid, partially surrounded by drapery. Below the miniature is the inscription "John Milton," and on two sides of the base of the pyramid bas reliefs representing the Expulsion and the Temptation. Standing against the pyramid is an oval representing the back of the miniature bearing upon it the following inscription:

> "This picture belong'd to Deborah Milton who was her Fathers Amannuensis at her death was sold to Sr Willm Davenants Family. it was painted by Mr Saml Cooper who was painter to Oliver Cromwell at ye time Milton was Latin Secratary to ye Protector.—The Painter & Poet were near of the same age, Milton was born in 1608 & died in 1674. Cooper was born in 1609 & died in 1672 & were—Companions & friends till Death parted Them. Several encouragers and Lovers of ye fine Arts / at that time wanted this picture. particularly Lord Dorset John Somers Esqr Sr Robt Howard Dryden Atterbury Dr Aldrich & Sr John Denham."

Beneath the base of the pyramid is inscribed:

> "The above is a fac simile of the manuscript on the back of the Picture, which appears to have been written sometime before the year 1693 when Mr. Somers was knighted, and afterwards created Baron Evesham, which brings it within nineteen years after Milton's death. The writer was

mistaken in supposing Deborah Milton to be dead at that time, she lived till 1727 but in indigence and obscurity married to a weaver in Spital Fields.

"I have only to add that Cooper appears to have exerted his utmost abilities on his friend's Picture, and that Miss Watson has shewn equal excellence in this specimen of her Art, the likeness to the original Picture which is in my possession is preserved with the utmost exactness.

J. REYNOLDS.
[Facsimile of signature]

Publish'd according to Act of Parliament, Jan^{ry} 4, 1786, by Caroline Watson, Fitzroy Street."
H. 8⅞. P.H. 2⅜. W. 6½. P.W. 1⅞.

151. There are proofs of this on India paper.
> Mentioned by Bromley.

152. CAROLINE WATSON, *engraver*.
(**142**) An oval, the same size as (**141**), inscribed: "Milton. Engraved by Caroline Watson, 1808. From a miniature by Cooper. Published Jan. 20, 1808, by Richard Philips."

153. BOUTROIS, *sculpt*.
(**143**) A similar print is inscribed: "J. Milton. Né en 1608. mort en 1674. Reynolds pinx." The mistake in the name of the artist is of course accounted for by Sir Joshua Reynolds' connection with the controversy.

(**144**) Mezzotint. Oval, 6 by 4¼ within the frame. Inscribed: "John Milton. Augsburg. By John Elias Haid."

154. COCHRAN, *sculpt*.
(**145**) A similar print is inscribed: "John Milton. Cooper del. Cochran sc." It was published in Bohn's edition of Milton's prose works, vol. I.
H. 7½. W. 5.

155. 145a. A variety of this portrait is inscribed: "John Milton. Engraved by J. Cochran. From a miniature painted by Mr. Saml Cooper, painter to Oliver Cromwell and originally in the possession of Milton's daughter

Deborah. London, I. J. Chidley, 123, Alderesgate Street." It is not known in what publication this illustration appeared. H. 8⅝. W. 5⅜.

(146) A print similar to **(145)** appears as a vignette to the edition of *L'Allegro* and *Il Penseroso* illustrated by Birkett Foster.

Du Roveray's Print

(147) A somewhat similar print inscribed: "Milton. Engraved by Wm Sharp after an original miniature by Samuel Cooper: the ornaments by G. B. Cipriani and E. F. Burney." The oval is surrounded with wreaths in front of a truncated column, against the base of which is an oval vignette representing the Temptation and measuring 3 by 2½. Published in Du Roveray's edition of *Paradise Lost,* 1802.
A proof impression is in the B.M.

156. 147a. A variety bears the additional inscription "London. Published by Verner Hood & Sharpe Poultry, 1808."

Craig's Drawing

(148) Oval in a landscape, above which is a crown of thorns in the sun and below a serpent, an apple and some roses. Inscribed: "John Milton. Drawn by W. M. Craig, Esqr., from a miniature by Cooper. R. Hicks sculp. Published by Nuttall, Fisher & Dixon, Liverpool, March 30, 1812."

157. HICKS, *sc.*
148a. Exactly similar to the above, but published by Henry Fisher, Caxton, London, 1823, instead of by Nuttall, Fisher & Dixon. The engraver's initial is not given. H. 8½. P.H. 3¼. W. 5¼. P.W. 2⅝.

Peck's Mezzotint

158. J. FABER, *fecit.*
(149) Half length in oval. Young man's portrait. Three-quarter face to the right. Long hair. Gown. White vest, open at neck. Inscribed:

"Iohannes Miltonus;
circa annum ætatis xxv^m.
Cedite Romani Scriptores, cedite Gran Propert.
Viro omatissimo Cuthberto Constable de Burton Constable in Com. Ebor,
Tabulam hanc merito votivam D.D.D. Francüs Peck, A.M."

H. 8½. S.H. 6¾. W. 6.
Published in Peck's *Memoirs*, 1740.
Mentioned by Bromley.

159. 149a. There are two states of this, one in black ink forming the frontispiece to the book and one in brown on rough paper.

ELDERTON MINIATURE

160. BASIRE, *sculpt*.

(**150**) Oval, in outline, 4½ by 1¾, forming one of a page of illustrations to the *Gentleman's Magazine*. Inscribed: "Picture supposed to be Milton. B(asire) sc."

VERTUE'S RICHARDSON PORTRAIT

(**151**) An oval, the frame of which terminates at the base in a foliated scroll in which is inserted a panel, and at the top a serpent, an apple, and lightning. Inscribed: "Ioannes Milton aetat 42. Ex musaeo J. Richardson. G. Vertuc sculpsit, 1751."
Size of plate 8¾ by 6.
There is an impression of this print in the B.M. and another in the Tangye collection.

THE CHESTERFIELD PORTRAIT

161. COOK, *sculpt*.

(**152**) Half length in oval. Three-quarter face to the left. Long hair, gown, white collar, white cuff, the right arm is resting on a book, the hand being raised to support the head. Above the oval is a ribbon and leaf ornament, and below is a tablet with rounded ends inscribed:

85

"John Milton."

The whole is set in a rectangular frame below which appears at the right the engraver's name and at the left "From an Original in Ld Chesterfield's Collection." Below is the inscription:

"Printed for John Bell near Exeter Exchange Strand London Novr 12th 1777."

H. 4¾. P.H. 2⅜. W. 2⅞. P.W. 2.

162. COOK, *sculpt.*

(**153**) Portrait of a young man with moustache, in gown, white collar, long hair, his head leaning on his hand in an attitude of thought. In an oval surmounted by a wreath tied with ribbon, and having below it a tablet on which is the name "John Milton." Inscribed:

"From an Original in Ld Chesterfield's Collection."

H. 5¾. P.H. 2⅜. W. 3⅞. P.W. 2.
The name tablet has square ends; (**152**) has the tablet with rounded ends.

(**154**) A copy of (**153**) with broader features. Appears in an edition of *Paradise Lost* published by Law, Millar & Co., London, 1792.

THE STRAWBERRY HILL PORTRAIT

163. S. HARDING, *del.* E. HARDING, JUN., *sculpt.*

(**155**) Half length figure in black velvet cavalier costume, with rich lace collar tied with tassels, and white under sleeves and lace cuffs. He has a pointed beard and moustache, and is in reclining attitude near a stone column. There is a landscape and tree in the distance. Inscribed:

"John Milton.
From an Original Picture in the Collection of Lord Orford, at Strawberry Hill. Published Decr 1 1796 by E. & S. Harding Pall Mall."

H. 9⅜. P.H. 7⅛. W. 6⅞. P.W. 6.
The same plate, published without date by Evans of Great Queen Street, figured as a portrait of Sir William Killigrew, "Vandyck pinx." being substituted for "S. Harding del." The original portrait belongs to the

Duke of Newcastle and is signed and dated 1638. It almost exactly corresponds with the print. There is no portrait of Killigrew mentioned in the Strawberry Hill sale, but a portrait of Milton does appear, Lot 7 in 21st day's sale.

THE CAPEL LOFFT PORTRAIT

164. P. V. PLAS, *fecit.*
   (**156**) Nearly three-quarter face, turning to the right. Near the figure is a pilgrim's staff with a bottle fastened to it. In the extreme upper right corner is a figure of the risen Saviour holding a banner, appearing on a beam of light. The poet is represented in a tightly buttoned coat and white collar. One hand rests upon the pedestal in front of him and the other is placed on the breast. Below the figure is a scroll showing in a somewhat illegible state the words "Inclitus et Felix Patriam"; and below it "P. V. Plas. Fec." Inscribed below the portrait:

> "P. V. Plas. Fecit.   Drawn & Engrav'd by G. Quinton.
> Milton.
> From an Original Picture in the possession of Capel Lofft, Esqr."
> "Publish'd August 1st 1797, by W. Stevenson, Norwich, for G. Quinton, Engraver & Sold by Messrs Boydell, Shakspeare Gallery, Pall Mall, London."

H. 12. P.H. 8¼. W. 9⅛. P.W. 6^{13}⁄$_{16}$.
The original portrait is in the National Portrait Gallery. It is suggested that it represents Bunyan rather than Milton.

165. (**157**) There is an enlarged copy on folio of the head from the preceding print, inscribed as follows: "Milton (from a picture by Plas) drawn on Stone by M. Gauci Esq. Printed by F. Moser, 4 Greenland Place, Cromer Street."

PORTRAIT IN DR. WILLIAMS'S LIBRARY

166. Drawn by J. THURSTON. Engraved by J. T. WEDGWOOD.
   (**158**) Nearly full face. Buttoned vest, gown, square Genevan collar showing lace end beneath, long hair. Inscribed:

"John Milton.

From a Picture by Dobson, in Dr Williams's Library. London, March 1
1820: Published by W. Walker, 8 Grays Inn Square. Printed by B. McQueen."

H. 7⅞. P.H. 3¹³⁄₁₆. W. 5⅜. P.W. 3¹⁄₁₆.

(N.B. The name of printer appears only on the proof impressions.)

This is the portrait of a coarse featured, heavy looking man, but there is no trace in his face of Milton's features.

PYE'S PRINT

167. (159) Portrait of a young man of about twenty or twenty-five, wearing an open waistcoat, black gown and white lace cravat. Long hair. Nearly full face. In a rectangle surrounded by a border of two lines. Inscribed: "John Milton. Painted by C. Janssen. Engraved by Charles Pye. London. Pubd for the Proprietor, March, 1823." Under the last line is a complex monogram which appears to be composed of the letters "T. W." The portrait does not in the least represent Milton and it is not known in what publication it appeared. Marsh refers to portraits uniform in style with it, representing John Locke, Louis XVI, William Pitt, George Washington, Algernon Sidney, Chancellor Thurlow, etc.

H. 7. P.H. 2¾. W. 5. P.W. 2.

PAGE'S PRINT

(160) There is a portrait in a suspended frame with ornamental corners, inscribed: "Milton. Engraved by R. Page from an original painting."

THE FALCONER MINIATURE

168. T. WOOLNOTH, *engraver.*

(161) Half length in oval. Three-quarter face to the right. Long hair, gown, white collar. Inscribed:

"John Milton.

From a Miniature of the same size by Faithorne, Anno 1667, in the possession of William Falconer Esq."

88

"Under the Superintendance of the Society for the Diffusion of Useful Knowledge."

"London, Published by Charles Knight, Pall Mall East."

H. 10. P.H. 2⅜. W. 6¾. P.W. 2⅛.

169. SAML. FREEMAN, *engraver*.

(**162**) Three-quarter face to the right. Buttoned vest, gown, square white collar showing tassels underneath, long hair. Inscribed:

"John Milton.
Engraved by Sam¹. Freeman, from a Miniature by Faithorne, Anno, 1667. Published by Archᵈ. Fullarton & Co. Glasgow."

H. 8¾. W. 5½.

This appeared in Cunningham's *Lives of Eminent and Illustrious Englishmen*, 8 vols. 8vo, Glasgow, 1835-7.

162a. There is a variety of the same portrait engraved by Holl in a rectangle with facsimile signature underneath, the above being a vignette.

170. 162b. Another variety reads A. Fullarton & Co., London and Edinburgh.

171. ANON. *engraver*.
(**163**) Half length, rectangular. Three-quarter face to the right. Long hair, gown, white collar. Inscribed "Milton."
H. 3. S.H. 2⅛. W. 2¼. S.W. 1⅝.

ANON. *engraver*.
(**164**) Rectangular. This was issued in the same plate with portraits of Barrow, Pope and Defoe, and was published by Routledge & Co. in Knight's *Half Hours with the best Authors*.
H. 3. P. H. 2⅛. W. 2¼. P.W. 1⅝.

PRINTS KNOWN TO MARSH BUT NEVER SEEN BY HIM

172. RIEDEL, *engraver*.
165. Portrait in an octagon. Inscribed:

"Riedel sc. Lips.
Milton.
Zwickau bei Gebr. Schumann."

H. 7⅝. P.H. 3⅜. W. 4⅝. P.W. 2¹³⁄₁₆.

166. There is a print in the B.M. of four ovals, representing Milton at four different periods of his life, each oval being 4 by 3½, inscribed:

"Joh H. Lips sculp. 1779."

173. 167. There is a title-page with vignette of Milton inscribed: "John Milton. Published Decr. 20, 1823, by G. Smeeton, Arcade, Pall Mall."
H. 5½. P.H. 2¼. W. 3½. P.W. 1¾.

174. D. COSTER, *sculpt.*

168. Marsh referred to a print he had never seen, closely resembling the Faithorne print (**24**) but much smaller in size. It is a finely engraved print and has Dryden's lines in script below the portrait with the poet's name and that of the engraver. It is exceedingly rare.
H. 5½. P.H. 3½. W. 3. P.W. 2¾.

VARIOUS ODD PRETENDED PORTRAITS

175. A. SMITH, *sculpt.*

169. Portrait in small oval. Inscribed: "A. Smith Sculpᵗ. From Faithorne. Published by Harrison & Co. Jan. 1, 1795."
H. 3. P.H. 1⅞. W. 2½. P.W. 1⁷⁄₁₆.

170. There is a rectangular print in the B. M. from Reidel's portrait inscribed: "Milton Engraved by C. Cook from a miniature by Faithorne. William Mackenzie, Glasgow Edinburgh London & New York." 5¼ by 4.

171. A variety is inscribed "Bosselman sc. Milton. Publié par Furne. Paris."

176. 172. Full length standing figure, representing a man with curly hair, dressed in a long cloak, knee breeches, stockings and shoes, with white bands about his neck. With one hand he gathers up his cloak and in the

90

other bears a roll. Background a village with trees. Inscribed: "Milton. J. Fougeron sculp."
H. 4¼. W. 2½.

177. 173. Portrait of a blind man with long hair. Head bent towards the left, one hand on breast, dark gown rolled about the shoulders. Inscribed: "Schubert Lith. Lith de Loux. Milton. Biographie univ. Album. Publie par H. Odé."
H. 9½. P.H. 3¾. W. 5½. P.W. 3.

178. 174. Full face portrait of a blind man. Black vest, gown, white collar tied with tassels, long hair. Inscribed: Milton. "Marckl d. Mad Ethiou."
H. 3½. W. 3½.

   175. There is a proof on India paper in the B.M. from the Cooper miniature portrait inscribed: "Verlag v. Franz Peley in Leipzig. Stich v. Druck v. Winkles & Lehmann in Leipzig."

179. 176. Line engraving without inscription. Half length figure of a man seated in a chair. Buttoned vest, gown, white collar tied with tassels, long hair. On the left is a column. 2½ by 2.

180. MAULET, *sculp.*
   177. There is a print inscribed "Milton," Publié par Furne a Paris Imp. F. Chardon, Hautefeuille.
3½ by 3½.

181. 178. There is an etching by C. W. Sherborn taken from the miniature in the possession of the Duke of Buccleuch, but not exactly resembling it.
Oval, 3 by 2½.

182. 179. Vertue's plate of Milton between Homer and Virgil should be alluded to. It is signed G. Vertue (G and V in monogram), *sc.*, and has Dryden's lines under the engraving.
H. 6½. P.H. 5½. W. 4.

183. 180. Lightbody's copy of the above is reversed and reduced, and to Dryden's lines the name of the author is not given.
H. 5½. P.H. 4¾. W. 3.

184. 181. Coloured print representing Milton's monument in St. Giles Church, Cripplegate. The monument is a bust set upon a pedestal, upon which are these words: "John Milton, author of Paradise Lost. Born Decr., 1608. Died Novr., 1674. His Father, John Milton, Died March 1646. They were both interred in this Church. Samuel Whitbread. J. Bacon sc."
H. 10. W. 7.

185. 182. There is a gravure of the Christ's College Bust, rectangular, brown ink.
H. 4¼. W. 3½.

N. B. *The numbers between 185 and 224 are left, in case of extra exhibits coming in at the last moment.*

MANUSCRIPTS

224. MINOR POEMS.
Lent by the Master and Fellows of Trinity College.
(*This will be exhibited only upon July* 10.)

225. THE BRIDGEWATER MANUSCRIPT OF COMUS.
Said to be in the handwriting of Henry Lawes.
Lent by the Earl of Ellesmere.

226. E. KING JUSTA (*Lycidas*). Cantab. 1638. 4°.
With MS. corrections by the author.
This will be exhibited only on July 10.
Lent by the University Library.

227. THE SAME.
Proof sheet with corrections for the press. This was discovered in the binding of a volume in the University Library by Mr. E. Burrell.
This will be exhibited only on July 10.
Lent by the University Library.

228. ORLANDO FURIOSO. Trans. Sir J. Harington.
With MS. notes by Milton.
Lent by the Rev. H. A. D. Surridge.

229. EURIPIDES. GENEVA, 1602.
With autograph signature of Milton[3], who bought it in 1634.
Lent by W. W. Vaughan, Esq.

---

[3] Milton's *Pindar* (Saumur, 1620) is in Harvard Library. His *Lycophron* is in New York. His *Aratus* (1559) is in the British Museum. See no. 86. (Information kindly supplied by Dr. J. E. Sandys.) The Euripides was once in Dr. Johnson's hands (S. Johnson, *Lives of the Poets*).

ON THE EARLY EDITIONS OF MILTON'S WORKS

POETICAL WORKS

The first edition of Milton's collected poems appeared in 1645. Previous to that time the poet had been known to most people chiefly as a prose pamphleteer. His lines *On Shakespeare*, written in 1630, were prefixed to the second folio Shakespeare in 1632, but anonymously. His *Comus*, written and acted in 1634, was sent to the press by his friend, Henry Lawes, in 1637[4], and his *Lycidas*, written in 1637, was printed in 1638[5] in the Cambridge University quarto volume of verses on the death of Edward King, but only bore the initials of the poet. The first group, therefore, of his poetical works is Moseley's octavo[6]. The volume was divided into two parts, the English and Italian poems, occupying 120 pages, coming first, and the Latin poems followed them. The title page to the book is as follows:—

"Poems of Mr. John Milton, both English and Latin, compos'd at several times. Printed by his true Copies. The Songs were set in Musick by Mr. Henry Lawes Gentleman of the King's Chappel, and one of His Maiesties Private Musick.

'Baccare frontem
Cingite, ne vati noceat mala lingua futuro.'
Virgil, Eclog. VII.

Printed and publish'd according to Order. London, Printed by Ruth Raworth for Humphrey Moseley, and are to be sold at the signe of the Princes Arms in Pauls Churchyard. 1645."

There was, however, a separate title printed for the Latin poems:—

"*Joannis Miltoni Londinensis Poemata: quorum pleraque intra annum aetatis vigesimum conscripsit: nunc primum edita. Londini, Typis R.R., Prostant ad Insignia Principis, in Caemeterio D. Pauli, apud Humphredum Moseley, 1645.*"

---

[4] See illustration.
[5] B. M. 239 k 36.
[6] B. M. E 1126.

and they were paged separately from 1 to 88 and arranged in two groups, the Elegies and the Sylvae. It was to this volume that the portrait by Marshall already referred to (see Catalogue of prints, No. (21)) was prefixed.

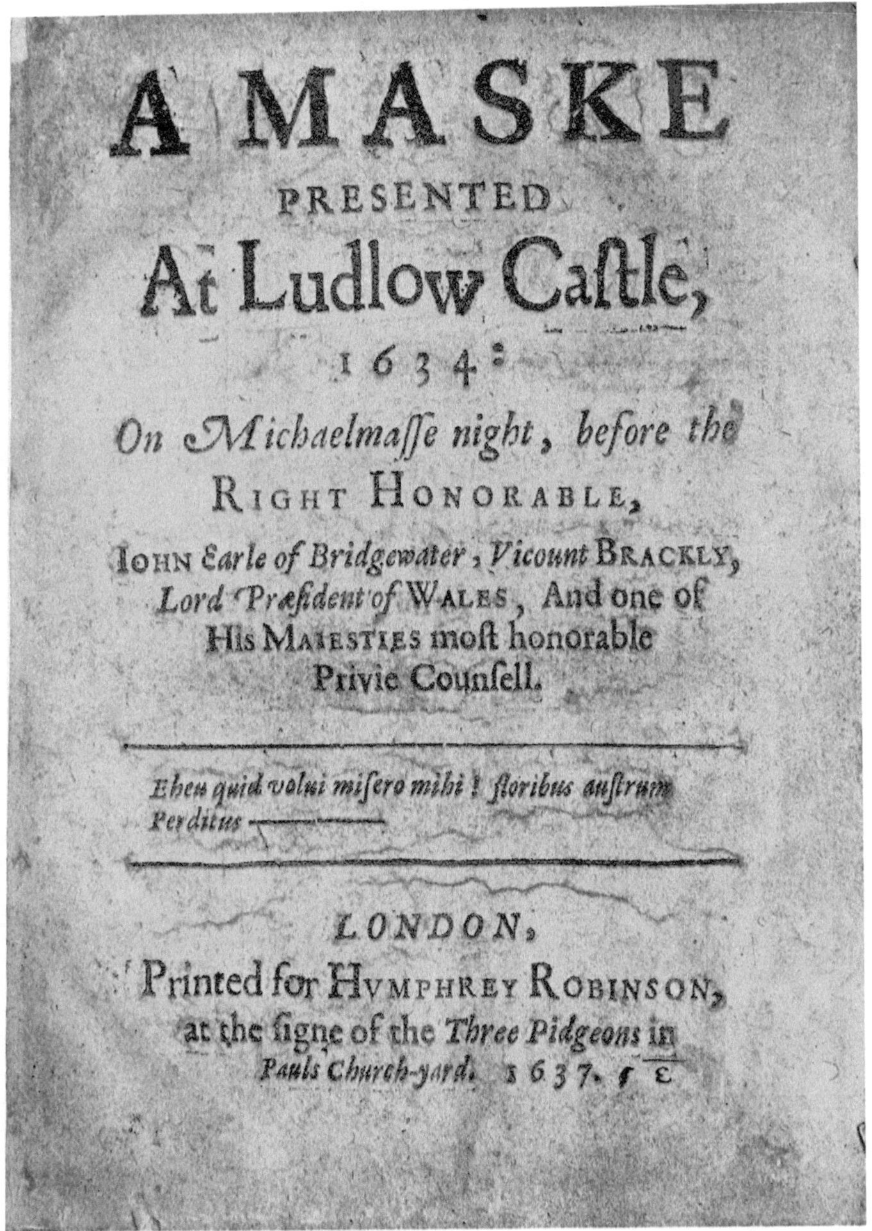

Full size facsimile of the title-page of the first edition of *Comus*.

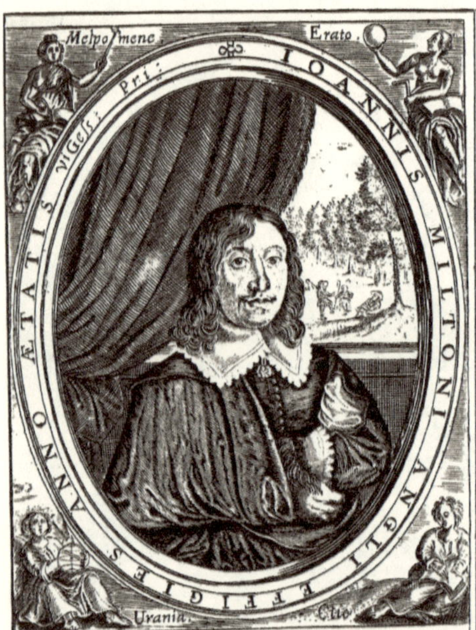

Title-page of the first collective edition of Milton's Minor Poems with the very
rare portrait by Marshall, 1645.

POEMS

OF

Mr. *John Milton*,

BOTH

ENGLISH and LATIN,

Compos'd at several times.

Printed by his true Copies.

The SONGS were set in Musick by
Mr. HENRY LAWES Gentleman of
the KINGS Chappel, and one
of His MAIESTIES
Private Musick.

——*Baccare frontem*
Cingite, ne vati noceat mala lingua futuro,
Virgil, Eclog. 7.

Printed and publish'd according to
ORDER.

LONDON,
Printed by *Ruth Raworth* for *Humphrey Moseley*,
and are to be sold at the signe of the Princes
Arms in S. *Pauls* Church-yard. 1645.

Full size facsimile of the title-page of the first collective edition of Milton's
Minor Poems, 1645.

Paradiſe loſt

A
POEM

Written in

TEN BOOKS

By *JOHN MILTON.*

Licenſed and Entred according
to Order.

LONDON

Printed; and are to be ſold by *Peter Parker*
under *Creed* Church neer *Aldgate*; And by
Robert Boulter at the *Turks Head* in *Biſhopſgate-ſtreet*;
And *Matthias Walker*, under St. *Dunſtons* Church
in *Fleet-ſtreet*, 1667.

Full size facsimile of the title-page of the first binding of the first
edition of *Paradise Lost*.

Paradise loſt.

A POEM

Written in

TEN BOOKS

By *JOHN MILTON.*

Licenſed and Entred according
to Order.

LONDON
Printed, and are to be ſold by *Peter Parker*
under *Creed* Church neer *Aldgate*; And by
Robert Boulter at the *Turks Head* in *Biſhopſgate-ſtreet*;
And *Matthias Walker*, under St. *Dunſtons* Church
in *Fleet-ſtreet*, 1667.

Full size facsimile of the title-page of the second binding of the first
edition of *Paradise Lost*.

Paradiſe loſt.

A
POEM
IN
TEN BOOKS

The Author _J. M._

Licenſed and Entred according
to Order.

LONDON

Printed, and are to be ſold by _Peter Parker_
under _Creed_ Church neer _Aldgate_ ; And by
Robert Boulter at the _Turks Head_ in _Biſhopſgate-ſtreet_ ;
And _Matthias Walker_, under St. _Dunſtons_ Church
in _Fleet-ſtreet_, 1668.

Full size facsimile of the title-page of the third binding of the third edition
of _Paradise Lost._

Paradiſe loſt.

A
POEM
IN
TEN BOOKS.

The Author
JOHN MILTON.

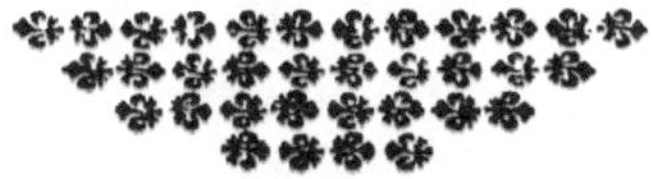

LONDON,
Printed by *S. Simmons,* and to be ſold by *S. Thomſon* at
the *Biſhopſ-Head* in *Duck-lane,* *H. Mortlack* at the
White Hart in *Weſtminſter* Hall, *M. Walker* under
St. *Dunſtans* Church in *Fleet ſtreet,* and *R. Boulter* at
the *Turk-Head* in *Biſhopſgate* ſtreet, 1668.

Full size facsimile of the title-page of the fifth binding of the first edition of
Paradise Lost.
The fourth binding resembled the third with some slight variations in the size of
the type.

In 1667 appeared the first edition of *Paradise Lost*[7], the title page of the first issue stating that the book was to be sold by "Peter Parker under Creed Church neer Aldgate; And by Robert Boulter at the Turk's Head in Bishopsgate Street; And Matthias Walker under St. Dunston's Church in Fleet Street." The printer was Simmons, but his name is not given, only those of the three booksellers whom he had employed to sell the book, and it is believed that the book was on sale in the last week of August, 1667. Its selling price was three shillings. It is a quarto volume of 342 pages, with good yellowish paper and legible type, and it was printed with remarkable accuracy. It had no argument or preface. Before the end of 1667 the first issued copies of the book seem to have been sold out, for there was a second binding that year and for this second issue a new title page, the wording exactly the same as before but the author's name in a smaller size of type. Professor Masson's numbering of the various bindings is adopted in the following statements. Early in 1668 a third binding of copies was issued, in which the author's initials only are given, the title page reading as follows:—

"Paradise lost. A Poem in Ten Books. The Author J. M. Licensed and Entred according to Order. London Printed, and are to be sold by Peter Parker under Creed Church neer Aldgate; And by Robert Boulter at the Turks Head in Bishopsgate-street; And Matthias Walker under St. Dunstons Church in Fleet-street, 1668."

This was followed in the same year by a fourth, with a title page identical to the above but with some slight variations in the size of the type, and a full stop after the word Books. In the fifth binding of the poem, with four rows of fleurs-de-lis under the author's name, issued also in 1668, appeared Milton's *Argument*, forming some introductory matter and giving a summary of the contents of the poem, and also a little prefatory paragraph entitled *The Verse*, this new matter filling fourteen pages and making the fifth binding a small quarto volume of 356 instead of 342 pages. The fifth title page read as follows:—

"Paradise lost. A Poem in Ten Books. The Author John Milton. London, Printed by S. Simmons, and to be sold by S. Thomson at the Bishops-Head in Duck-Lane, H. Mortlack at the White Hart in Westminster Hall, M Walker under St. Dunstons Church in Fleet-street, and R. Boulter at the Turks-Head in Bishopsgate-street, 1668."

---

[7] See illustration.

The full name of the author was restored to it and Simmons put his name upon the title page, declaring himself as the printer and publisher. One of the three former booksellers, Peter Parker, was employed no longer and the names of two new booksellers appear. There is one other curious feature respecting this fifth binding. Simmons himself had written a four-line advertisement to introduce the new matter and this was at first set up as follows:—

"*The Printer to the Reader. Courteous Reader,* There was no Argument at first intended to the Book, but for the satisfaction of many that have desired it, is procured. *S. Simmons.*"

But before the requisite number of copies of the fourteen pages were wholly printed off Milton had corrected the grammatical errors made by his printer and had amended the advertisement as follows:—

"*The Printer to the Reader. Courteous Reader,* There was no Argument at first intended to the Book, but for the satisfaction of many that have desired it, I have procur'd it, and withall a reason of that which stumbled many others, why the Poem Rimes not. *S. Simmons.*"

Some copies therefore of the fifth binding have Simmons' incorrect form of the advertisement and some Milton's amended form. In the sixth binding, again issued in 1668, there is another title page differing from the last, however, in nothing essential, but in a few details of ornamentation, as it has three stars before and after the author's name; but in the seventh binding, which appeared in 1669, there is a fresh title page altogether. The year appears for the first time and only one bookseller's name is mentioned, the title being as follows:—

"*Paradise lost. A Poem in Ten Books. The Author John Milton. London, Printed by S. Simmons, and are to be sold by T. Helder, at the Angel, in Little Brittain, 1669.*"

There were, Masson states, two more bindings of the book in that same year, the eighth and the ninth, and the title pages of these are exactly the same in wording as the last, but differ from it in small details of lettering and pointing; "angel" being in italics and a comma taking the place of a full stop after "Brittain." The exact divergence between Masson's eighth and ninth title pages is not very clear. Before the end of April, 1669, the first edition of the poem had been exhausted, about 1,300 copies having been sold in little more than eighteen months.

This Indenture Made the 27th day of Aprill 1667 Betweene John Milton gent of the one ptie
And Samuell Symons Printer of thother ptie Wittnesse That the said John Milton in consideracion
of five pounds to him now paid by the said Samll Symons and other the consideracions herein
menconed hath given granted and assigned, and by these pents doth give grant & assigne
unto the said Samll Symons his Executors and assignes All that Booke Copy or
Manuscript of a Poem intituled Paradise lost, or by whatsoever other title or name
the same is or shalbe called or distinguished now lately Licensed to be printed
Togather with the full benefitt proffitt & advantage thereof or wch shall or may
arise thereby And the said John Milton for him his exec & adm doth covenant wth
the said Samll Symons his ex & ass That he and they shall at all tymes
hereafter have hold and enioy the same and all Impressions thereof accordingly
wthout the lett or hinderance of him the said John Milton his ex adm or ass or any
or ass by his or their consent or privitie, And that he the said Jo. Milton his ex
or ass or any other by his or their meanes or consent shall not print or cause
to be printed or sell dispose or publish the said Booke or Manuscript or
any other Booke or Manuscript of the same tenor or subiect wthout the consent of
the said Samll Symons his ex & ass In consideracion whereof the said Samll
Symons for him his ex & ass doth covenant wth the said John Milton his ex & ass
well and truly to pay unto the said John Milton his ex & ass the sum of five
pounds of lawfull english money at the end of the first Impression which the said

The original agreement for the publication of *Paradise Lost*, from the British Museum.

Paradiſe loſt.

A
POEM
IN
TEN BOOKS

The Author
JOHN MILTON.

LONDON,
Printed by S. Simmons, and are to be ſold by
T. Helder, at the *Angel* in *Little Brittain*,
1 6 6 9.

Full size facsimile of the title-page of the seventh binding of the first edition
of *Paradise Lost*.

Paradiſe loſt.

A POEM

IN

TEN BOOKS.

The Author
JOHN MILTON.

LONDON,
Printed by *S. Simmons*, and are to be ſold by
T. Helder at the Angel in *Little Brittain.*
1 6 6 9.

Full size facsimile of the title-page of the eighth binding of the first edition
of *Paradise Lost.*

PARADISE REGAIN'D.

A POEM.

In IV BOOKS.

To which is added

SAMSON AGONISTES.

The Author
JOHN MILTON.

LONDON,

Printed by *J. M* for *John Starkey* at the
Mitre in *Fleetstreet*, near *Temple-Bar*.
MDCLXXI.

Full size facsimile of the title-page of the first edition of *Paradise Regained*.

SAMSON AGONISTES,

A

DRAMATIC POEM.

The Author
J O H N   M I L T O N.

Ariſtot. Poet. Cap. 6.

Τεαγῳδία μίμησις πεάξεως σπεδαίας, &c.

Tragœdia eſt imitatio actionis ſeriæ, &c. Per miſericordiam &
metum perficiens talium affectuum luſtrationem.

LONDON,

Printed by *J. M.* for *John Starkey* at the
Mitre in *Fleetſtreet*, near *Temple-Bar.*
MDCLXXI.

I

Full size facsimile of the title-page of the first edition of *Samson Agonistes.*

POEMS, &c.

UPON

Several Occasions.

BY
Mr. *JOHN MILTON*:

Both E N G L I S H and L A T I N, &c.
Compofed at feveral times.

With a fmall Tractate of
EDUCATION
To Mr. HARTLIB

LONDON,
Printed for *Tho. Dring* at the *Blew Anchor*
next *Mitre Court* over againft *Fetter*
Lane in *Fleet-ftreet*. 1673.

Full size facsimile of the title-page of the second edition of the Poems.

Paradiſe Loſt.

A
POEM
IN
TWELVE BOOKS.

The Author
JOHN MILTON.

The Second Edition
Reviſed and Augmented by the
ſame Author.

LONDON,
Printed by *S. Simmons* next door to the
Golden Lion in Alderſgate-ſtreet, 1674.

The second edition of *Paradise Lost*.

In 1671 appeared the first edition[8] of Paradise Regained. It was licensed on July 2nd, 1670, and may perhaps have appeared in that year although it is dated in the following year. The volume was an octavo of 220 pages, the first 112 of which after the general title page contained *Paradise Regained*, while the remainder, with a special title page and the pages separately numbered, contained *Samson Agonistes*. The paper was thick and the type rather large, but the printing slovenly and the pointing careless throughout and sometimes very bad. The title page was as follows:—

"Paradise Regain'd. A Poem. In IV Books. To which is added Samson Agonistes. The Author John Milton. London, Printed by J. M. for John Starkey at the Mitre in Fleetstreet, near Temple-Bar. MDCLXXI."

The separate one to Samson Agonistes reads:—

"Samson Agonistes, A Dramatic Poem. The Author John Milton.—Aristot. Poet. Cap. 6. Τραγῳδία μίμησις πράξεως σπουδαίας &c. &c. Tragædia est imitatio actionis seriæ, &c. Per misericordiam et metum perficiens talium affectuum lustrationem.—London, Printed by J. M. for John Starkey at the Mitre in Fleetstreet, Near Temple-Bar. MDCLXXI."

In 1673 there appeared a new edition of the minor poems:—

"Poems, &c., upon Several Occasions. By Mr. John Milton: Both English and Latin, &c. Composed at several times. With a small Tractate of Education to Mr. Hartlib. London, Printed for Tho. Dring at tke White Lion next Chancery Lane End, in Fleet-street, 1673."

But there are two imprints, one as we have just given it and the other reading:—

"for Tho. Dring at the Blew Anchor next Mitre Court over against Fetter Lane in Fleet-street, 1673."

The volume was an octavo, containing 290 pages, the Latin poems following the English with a separate title page and numbering of the pages, and a reprint of the Tractate to Hartlib coming at the end. In some copies there is a representation of Dolle's reduction of the Faithorne portrait used in the *Treatise on Logic*. This second edition was of course merely a reprint of the

---

[8] B. M. 684 d 33.

first edition of 1645, but the preface, Lawes' dedication of the *Comus* and Wotton's letter in praise of *Comus* were omitted, while nine more sonnets were added, several translations, and two juvenile poems by Milton entitled *On the death of a Fair Infant dying of a cough*, and *At a Vacation Exercise in the College*. There were certain Latin additions, but the portrait was not reproduced although the epigram re-appeared with the heading *In Effigiei ejus sculptorem*.

A new edition of *Paradise Lost* appeared in 1674 with the title:—

"Paradise Lost. A Poem In Twelve Books. The Author John Milton. The Second Edition Revised and Augmented by the same Author. London, Printed by S. Simmons next door to the Golden Lion in Aldersgate-street. 1674."

It was small octavo, and some copies contained Dolle's portrait reduced in 1671 from the Faithorne engraving. The pages were numbered, the argument distributed throughout the volume, and there were eight extra lines added to those which appeared in the first edition, three to open Book VIII and five to open Book XII. Two sets of commendatory verses were prefixed, one set in Latin by Samuel Barrow, the other in English by Andrew Marvell.

These constituted all the editions of the poetical works issued during Milton's life.

PROSE WORKS

The first of Milton's pamphlets to appear was a small quarto of 90 pages issued in 1641, bearing this title:—

"Of Reformation touching Church Discipline in England and the Causes that hitherto have hindered it: Two Books, written to a Friend: printed for Thomas Underhill, 1641."

It was issued anonymously, and we do not know who was the "Friend" to whom the two books composing the pamphlet were addressed. It is not known exactly in what month it appeared, but the general decision is that it appeared after May 12.

The second pamphlet was also anonymous, but there are copies of it in existence with Milton's name inserted in the title page by contemporary hands, and on one copy, in the British Museum, the name is believed to have been written in by the author himself. It was a pamphlet in small quarto size of 24 pages, bearing the following title:—

"Of Prelatical Episcopacy, and whether it may be deduc'd from the Apostolical times by vertue of those testimonies which are alleg'd to that purpose in some late Treatises; one whereof goes under the name of James, Archbishop of Armagh. London: Printed by R. O. and G. D. for Thomas Underhill, and are to be sold at the signe of the Bible in Wood Street: 1641."

All but simultaneously with it appeared a third, which is not registered at Stationers' Hall, but is believed to have appeared in July, 1641. It also was anonymous, and consisted of 68 small quarto pages[9], introduced by an apologetic preface. The title reads:—

"Animadversions upon the Remonstrant's Defence against Smectymnuus. London: Printed for Thomas Underhill, and are to be sold at the signe of the Bible in Wood Street: 1641."

The fourth anti-episcopal pamphlet was a quarto[10] of 55 pages, issued in 1641, with title:—

"The Reason of Church-government urg'd against Prelaty, by Mr. John Milton: In two Books: London, Printed by E. G. for John Rothwell, and are to be sold at the Sunne in Paul's Churchyard, 1641."

The fifth[11] was issued in March or April, 1642, and this consisted of 55 pages in small quarto. The title was as follows:—

"An Apology against a Pamphlet call'd A Modest Confutalion of the Animadversions of the Remonstrant against Smectymnuus: London, Printed by E. G. for John Rothwell, and are to be sold at the Signe of the Sunne in Paul's Churchyard, 1642."

Milton's first divorce tract[12] was in print and on sale in London on the 1st August, 1643. The title on the copy in the British Museum reads as follows:—

---

[9] B. M. E 166 (11).

[10] B. M. E 137 (9).

[11] B. M. E 147 (22).

[12] B. M. E 62 (17).

and there is a manuscript note on it "Written by John Milton," and another one, "August 1st," showing that to the collector of this particular copy, Thomason, the facts as to its issue were well known. It was a pamphlet of 48 quarto pages, with an extra page supplying two omitted passages, and the text was printed continuously without division into chapters. The second edition of it[13] appeared on February 2nd, 1643-4, with this new title:—

Underneath this title the text Matth. xiii. 52 is repeated from the title of the first edition, with new text added, Prov. xviii. 13: "He that answereth a matter before he heareth it, it is folly and shame unto him." Then follows the imprint, "*London, Imprinted in the yeare 1644.*" It is a small quarto of 88 pages, the text divided into two books, each of which is subdivided into chapters, and having an introductory letter, consisting of six pages, addressed "*To the Parliament of England, with the Assembly,*" signed in full John Milton.

The celebrated tract on Education, a thin quarto[14] of eight pages in rather small type without a title page, but entitled "Of Education to Master Samuel Hartlib," made its appearance on June 5th, 1644. It was published by Thomas Underhill of Wood Street, who had published Milton's first three anti-episcopal pamphlets, and, although it had no author's name, the copy in the British Museum bears a note written by Thomason to the effect that Milton was the author, and giving the date of the publication. This was the tract to which we have already referred as reprinted in 1673 at the end of the second

---

[13] B. M. E 31 (5) and see 117 i 59.
[14] B. M. E 50 (12).

edition of Milton's minor poems[15], and on that occasion the words "Written above twenty years since" were added to the original title.

A further tract on divorce came out on the 15th July, 1644, five weeks after the publication of the tract on education, and five and a half months after the appearance of the second edition of the *Doctrine and Discipline of Divorce*. It consisted of 40 small quarto pages[16], of which, however, only 24 are numbered, these 24 consisting of abridged translations by Milton of certain passages from Martin Bucer. They are preceded by six pages of "Testimonies of the high approbation which learned men have given of Martin Bucer," and then by eight pages of closer type addressed by Milton to the Parliament and signed with his name in full. At the end, after the numbered pages, there is a postscript of two pages in which Milton again speaks directly and winds up the tract. The title page is as follows, and it will be noticed that it does not mention the name of the author of the tract:—

"The judgement of Martin Bucer concerning Divorce. Writt'n to Edward the Sixt, in his Second Book of the Kingdom of Christ. And now English. Wherein a late Book restoring the Doctrine and Discipline of Divorce, is heer confirm'd and justify'd by the authoritie of Martin Bucer. To the Parlament of England. John 3. 10: Art thou a teacher in Israel, and know'st not these things? Publisht by Authoritie. London, Printed by Matthew Simmons, 1644."

The great controversy then arose respecting the liberty of the press, and on November 24th, 1644, appeared Milton's celebrated work *Areopagitica*. It was a small quarto[17] of 40 pages with the following title:—

AREOPAGITICA: A Speech of Mr. John Milton for the Liberty of Unlicens'd Printing, to the Parlament of England.

Τοὐλεύθερον δ' ἐκεῖνο, εἴ τις θέλει πόλει

Χρηστόν τι βούλευμ' εἰς μέσον φέρειν, ἔχων.

Καὶ ταῦθ' ὁ χρήζων, λαμπρὸς ἔσθ, ὁ μὴ θέλων,

Σιγᾷ, τί τούτων ἐστιν ἰσαίτερον πόλει;

Euripid. Hicetid.

---

[15] B. M. 684 d 34.

[16] B. M. 883 g 4.

[17] B. M. E 18 (9) and see 713 f 11 (1) and G 608.

> This is true Liberty, when free-born men
> Having to advise the public may speak free,
> Which he who can, and will, deserv's high praise,
> Who neither can nor will, may hold his peace;
> What can be juster in a State than this?

Euripid. Hicetid.

London, Printed in the yeare 1644.

It had no printer's or publisher's name attached to it.

Shortly afterwards were issued two new divorce treatises, neither of them licensed or registered, and both appearing on one day, March 4th, 1644-5. The first is the *Tetrachordon*, a treatise[18] consisting of 104 small quarto pages, of which six, not numbered, are occupied with a dedication to Parliament and the remaining 98 are numbered and form the body of the work. The following is the full title:—

TETRACHORDON: Expositions upon The foure chief places in Scripture, which treat of Marriage, or nullities in Marriage.

On Gen. i. 27-28, compar'd and explain'd by Gen. ii. 18, 23, 24.

Deut. xxiv. 1-2.

Matth. v. 31-32, with Matth. xix., from the 3 v. to the 11th.

1 Cor. vii., from the 10th to the 16th.

Wherin the Doctrine and Discipline of Divorce, as was lately publish'd, is confirm'd by explanation of Scripture, by testimony of ancient Fathers, of civill lawes in the Primitive Church, of famousest Reformed Divines, and lastly, by an intended Act of the Parlament and Church of England in the last yeare of Edward the Sixth. By the former Author J. M.

> —Σκαιοῖσι καινὰ προσφέρων σοφά
> Δόξεις ἀχρεῖος, κ' οὐ σοφὸς πεφυκέναι·
> Τῶν δ' αὖ δοκούντων εἰδέναι τι ποικίλον,
> Κρείσσων νομισθεὶς ἐν πόλει λυπρός φανῇ.

Euripid. Medea.

London: Printed in the yeare 1645.

---

[18] B. M. E 271 (12) and see 108 b 53 and 5175 c (2) *with notes,* and 498 b 32 and G 19594 (2).

The other is the *Colasterion*, a short tract[19] of 27 pages, without a preface, having the following title:—

> *"A Reply to a Nameles Answer against 'The Doctrine and Discipline of Divorce.' Wherein the trivial Author of that Answer is discovver'd, the Licenser conferr'd with, and the Opinion which they traduce defended. By the former author, J. M.* Prov. xxvi. 5, Answer a Fool according to his folly, lest hee bee wise in his own conceit. *Printed in the year* 1645."

During the King's trial Milton had been busy preparing a pamphlet signifying his unqualified adhesion to a republican form of government, and in 1649 this pamphlet appeared, four days after the publication of the *Eikon Basilike*. It was a small quarto of 42 pages, unlicensed and printed by Matthew Simmons, who had been the publisher of Milton's Bucer tract, and it came out exactly a fortnight after the death of the King and a week after the declaration of a republic. Its title[20] was as follows:—

> *"The Tenure of Kings and Magistrates: proving, That it is Lawfull, and hath been held so through all Ages, for any, who have the Power, to call to account a Tyrant, or wicked King, and after due conviction, to depose, and put him to death; if the ordinary Magistrate have neglected, or deny'd to doe it. And that they, who of late, so much blame Deposing are the Men that did it themselves. The Author, J. M. London, Printed by Matthew Simmons, at the Gilded Lyon in Aldersgate Street,* 1649."

The *Eikon Basilike*, issued February 9, 1649, had circulated in many thousands of copies and had created great excitement. Milton's answer[21] to it appeared on October 6, 1649, with the following very lengthy title page:—

> "ΕΙΚΟΝΟΚΛΑΈΣΤΗΣ in Answer To a Book Intitl'd ἘΙΚΩΊΝ ΒΑΣΙΛΙΚΉ. The Portraiture of his Sacred Majesty in his Solitudes and sufferings. The Author I. M.
>
> Prov. xxviii. 15, 16, 17.
> 15. As a roaring Lyon, and a ranging Beare, so is a wicked Ruler over the poor people.

---

[19] B. M. 271 (11).
[20] B. M. E 542 (12).
[21] B. M. E 578 (5).

16. The Prince that wanteth understanding, is also a great oppressor; but he that hateth covetousnesse shall prolong his dayes.

17. A man that doth violence to the blood of any person, shall fly to the pit, let no man stay him.

Salust. Conjurat. Catilin.

Regium imperium, quod initio, conservandae libertatis, atque augendae reipub. causâ fuerat, in superbiam, dominationemque se convertit.

Regibus boni, quam mali, suspectiores sunt; semperque his aliena virtus formidolosa est.

Quidlibet impunè facere, hoc scilicet regium est.

Published by Authority.

London, Printed by Matthew Simmons, next dore to the gilded Lyon in Aldersgate street. 1649."

It is marked by very direct personal and savage antipathy to Charles and by an intensely strong expression of the sentiment of anti-royalism.

The new edition of *Eikonoklastes* came out in 1650, a quarto[22] consisting of 230 pages, enlarged upon the first edition but closer printed, so that it had fewer pages, the first having 242 and this one 230. Its title is as follows:—

"ΕΙΚΟΝΟΚΛΑΣΤΗΣ, *in Answer to a Book Intitl'd The Portraiture of his Sacred Majesty in his Solitudes and Sufferings. The Author I. M.*

Prov. xxviii. 15, 16, 17.

15. *As a roaring Lyon, and a ranging Beare, so is a wicked Ruler over the poor people.*

16. *The Prince that wanteth understanding, is also a great oppressor; but he that hateth covetousnesse shall prolong his dayes.*

17. *A man that doth violence to the blood of any person, shall fly to the pit, let no man stay him.*

Salust. Conjurat. Catilin.

Regium imperium, quod initio, conservandae libertatis, atque augendae reipub. causâ fuerat, in superbiam, dominationemque se convertit.

---

[22] B. M. 599 e 18 (1).

Regibus boni, quam mali, suspectiores sunt; semperque his aliena virtus formidolosa est.

Impunè quaelibet facere, id est Regem esse.—Idem Bell. Jugurth.

Publish'd now the Second time, and much Enlarg'd. London, Printed by T. N., and are to be sold by Tho. Brewster and G. Moule at the three Bibles in Pauls Church-yard near the West-End, 1650."

About this time arose the controversy with Salmasius, and Milton had been instructed by the Commonwealth to answer the book "written by Salmasius against the proceedings of the Commonwealth." His answer appeared in 1650 according to the imprint but the book does not seem to have been on sale till March, 1651. It was in a printed duodecimo[23] of 260 pages of text with index. It was in Latin only, although it had been registered as to appear in both Latin and English on the 31st December, 1650. Its title reads:—

"Joannis Miltoni Angli pro Populo Anglicano Defensio, contra Claudii Anonymi, alias Salmasii, Defensionem Regiam: Cum Indice. Londini, Typis Dugardianis, Anno Domini 1651."

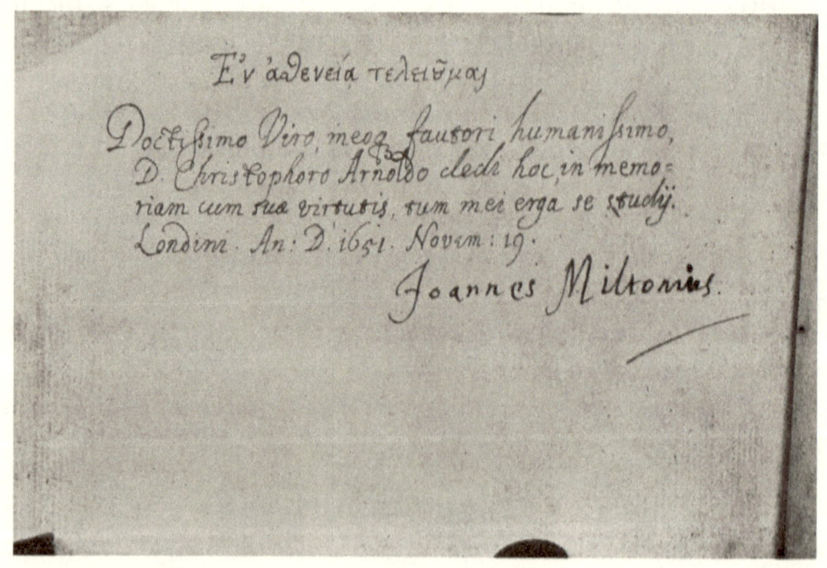

Signature of John Milton, 19 Nov. 1651, written in the Album Amicorum of Christopher Arnold, Professor of History at Nuremberg, now preserved in the British Museum.

---

[23] B. M. 1650 edit 8133 a 5 (1); 1651 edit 521 a 16 (2) and E 1393 and others.

It may be recorded at this place that although not actually a publication, Arnold's Album, now in the British Museum, contained Milton's contribution made during 1651. It takes the form of a modified quotation from 2 Cor. xii. 9 in the Greek, thus: "Εν ἀσθενείᾳ τελειοῦμαι," with a Latin sequel to this effect: "To the very learned Mr. Christopher Arnold, my most obliging friend, I have given this, in memory both of his own worth and of my regard for him. London. A.D. 1651. Novem: 19. Joannes Miltonius." Only the signature seems to be in Milton's hand, the Greek motto and the Latin inscription having been first written very elegantly from his dictation, to receive his signature.

We now come to an interesting pamphlet which is generally accepted as being the work of Milton. It appeared in May 1653, a thin pamphlet of 20 pages with this title:—

"A Letter to a Gentleman in the Country, touching the Dissolution of the late Parliament and the Reasons thereof.... London, printed by F. Leach, for Richard Baddeley, at his shop within the Middle Temple Gate, 1653."

Although signed N. LL. there is almost definite proof, corroborated by the inscription on the Thomason copy in the British Museum "By Mr. John Milton," that it was from his pen.

His next serious work was the *Defensio Secunda*, a small octavo volume[24] of 173 pages published in London, May 30th, 1654. Its title reads:—

"Joannis Miltoni Angli pro Populo Anglicano Defensio Secunda. Contra infamem libellum anonymum cui titulus, Regii sanguinis clamor ad caelum adversus parricidas Anglicanos.' Londini, Typis Neucomianis, 1654."

Although not actually issued by Milton himself it is right to mention the edition of this book which appeared in The Hague. It was a volume[25] in two parts, Milton's *Defensio Secunda* filling 128 pages, and another work, More's *Fides Publica*, the latter part of the book and extending to 129 pages separately numbered. Its preliminary matter consisted of two prefaces, one headed *"Lectori,"* and the other, the Printer's statement, *"Typographus pro Se-ipso."* Its full title page is as follows:—

---

²⁴ B. M. 599 a 23 and E 1487 (3).

²⁵ B. M. 600 a 12 (1). See also 848 b 10.

"Joannis Miltoni Defensio Secunda pro Populo Anglicano contra infamem Libellum cujus titulus 'Regii Sanguinis Clamor adversus Parricidas Anglicanos.' Accessit Alexandri Mori, Ecclesiastae, Sacrarumque Litterarum Professoris, Fides Publica contra calumnias joannis Miltoni, Scurrae. Hagae-Comitum, ex Typographia Adriani Ulac, MDCLIV."

Then came Milton's rejoinder to the work of More, *Fides Publica* just named. It is a small volume[26] of 204 pages, entitled:—

"Joannis Miltoni, Angli, Pro Se Defensio contra Alexandrum Morum, Ecclesiasten, Libelli famosi, cui titulus 'Regii Sanguinis Clamor ad Caelum adversus Parricidas Anglicanos,' authorem recte dictum. Londini, Typis Neucomianis, 1655."

It was issued in Latin only and it has never, so far as we know, been translated into English.

Of the *Defensio Prima* a fresh edition[27] appeared in October 1658, just after the death of Oliver Cromwell. It is an octavo book well printed and has hardly any variations from the first edition, save the addition of a very important postscript which fills two pages. The full title reads:—

"Joannis Miltonii, Angli, Pro Populo Anglicano Defensio contra Claudii Anonymi, alias Salmasii, Defensionem Regiam. Editio correctior et auctior, ab Autore denuo recognita. Londini, Typis Neucombianis, Anno Dom. 1658."

Following it came a small tract[28], a very tiny octavo, the address to the Parliament filling ten pages and bearing the author's signature in full and the actual tract following it with 83 pages. It was called:—

"A Treatise of Civil Power in Ecclesiastical Causes: Shewing that it is not lawfull for any power on Earth to compell in matters of Religion. The author J. M. London, Printed by Tho. Newcomb, Anno 1659."

This, it was intimated, was but the first of two tracts and the other was to follow. It appeared, a small octavo volume[29], in the same year, containing 18

---

[26] B. M. E 1661 (2).
[27] B. M. E 1900 (1).
[28] B. M. 1019 b 18.
[29] B. M. E 2110 (2).

unnumbered pages of an address to the Parliament printed in large type, these being followed by 153 pages of text. The tract was the second one on Disestablishment and had this title:—

"Considerations touching the likeliest means to remove Hirelings out of the Church. Wherein is also discoure'd of Tithes, Church-fees, Church Revenues; and whether any maintenance of ministers can be settl'd by law. The author J. M. London, Printed by T. N. for L. Chapman at the Crown in Popes-head Alley, 1659."

Almost at the same time Milton wrote a *Letter to a Friend concerning the Ruptures of the Commonwealth*. It is dated Oct. 20, 1659, but it was not printed until 1698, and then appeared in the so-called Amsterdam Edition[30] of Milton's Works. A somewhat similar experience was the fate of a private letter to General Monk which bears no date but belongs to 1660. It was called:—

"The Present Means and Brief Delineation of a Free Commonwealth, easy to be put in practice and without delay: In a Letter to General Monk."

and consisted of but three pages and it came later on into Toland's hands and was passed on by him for use in the 1698 edition[31] of the Prose Works.

The "Readie and Easie Way," one of the most notable of Milton's pamphlets[32], a small quarto of 18 pages, came out in March 1659-60, and Thomason's copy bears date March 3. Its full title read:—

"The Readie and Easie Way to Establish a Free Commonwealth, and the Excellence therof compar'd with the inconveniences and dangers of readmitting kingship in this nation. The author J. M. London, Printed by T. N., and are to be sold by Livewell Chapman at the Crown in Popes-Head Alley. 1660."

The same year witnessed his bitter attack on Dr. Griffith for his Royalist sermon, a short and exceedingly rare pamphlet[33] called:—

"Brief Notes upon a late Sermon, titled 'The Fear of God and the King'; Preach'd, and since publish'd, by Matthew Griffith, D.D., and Chaplain to the late

---

[30] B. M. 713 k 8.

[31] See note 30

[32] B. M. E 1016 (11).

[33] No copy in the B. M.

This being followed by a second and enlarged edition of the "Ready and Easy Way." It was practically a new work, having large additions to the preceding issue, many omissions, many changes of phraseology. Among the additions the most prominent is this motto (an extension of Juvenal 1. 15, 16) prefixed to the whole:—

*"Et nos
Consilium dedimus Syllae: demus Populo nunc."*

Then follows a long period covered by the issue of *Paradise Lost*, and the next publication after that of the great poem was a work of a very different sort. It was a Latin Grammar[34] called:—

"Accedence Commenc't Grammar, Supply'd with sufficient Rules, For the use of such (Younger or Elder) as are desirous, without more trouble than needs to attain the Latin Tongue, The Elder sort especially, with little Teaching and their own Industry, By John Milton. London, Printed for S. S. and are to be sold by John Starkey at the Miter in Fleet-street, near Temple-bar, 1669."

A small duodecimo consisting of two pages of preliminary address "To the Reader," and 65 pages of text with some errata at the end. The publisher, S. S., was probably Samuel Simmons, but Milton may have paid the cost of printing himself, as the imprint seems to imply.

The *History of Britain*, the work in which Faithorne's excellent portrait appeared, followed the Latin Grammar very speedily. It was a quarto[35] of 308 pages with an Index of 52 unnumbered pages more, and was called:—

"The History of Britain, That part especially now call'd England. From the first Traditional Beginning, continu'd to the Norman Conquest. Collected out of the antientest and best Authours thereof by John Milton. London, Printed by J. M. for James Allestry, at the Rose and Crown in St Paul's Church Yard, MDCLXX."

---

[34] B. M. 12935 a 30, also see 624 a 34 (3) and G 16707.
[35] B. M. 598 e 1.

Quickly upon its heels came the Latin work on Logic[36], an ill printed duodecimo of 235 pages with this title:—

"Joannis Miltoni Angli, Artis Logicae Plenior Institutio, ad Petri Rami Methodum Concinnata, Adjecta est Praxis Annalytica [sic] et Petri Rami Vita. Libris duobus. Londini, Impensis Spencer Hickman, Societatis Regalis Typographi, ad insigne Rosae in Cœmeterio D. Pauli. 1672."

and having affixed to it a reduction of the Faithorne portrait, re-engraved at the reduced scale by W. Dolle.

Of the new edition of the Minor Poems which came out in 1673 we have already spoken, but the fruit of that year included a prose work also. It was a quarto tract[37] of 16 pages called:—

"Of True Religion, Haeresie, Schism, Toleration, And what best means may be us'd against the growth of Popery. The Author J. M. London, Printed in the year, 1673."

and had no printer's or publisher's name and the initials only of the author. The last page is in smaller type than the rest, and the appearance of the whole tract betokens haste, risk and possible evasion of the law. It was certainly an irregular and unlicensed issue.

It was at this time that the Letter on Education addressed to Hartlib was reprinted for inclusion in the new edition of the Minor Poems with its author's name attached to it.

We now approach the end, and the final work[38] to appear during the lifetime of the author is called:—

"Joannis Miltoni Angli, Epistolarum Familiarium Liber Unus: Quibus accesserunt, Ejusdem, jam olim in Collegio Adollescentis, Prolusiones Quaedam Oratoriae. Londini, Impensis Brabazoni Aylmeri sub signo Trium Columbarum, Via vulgo Cornhill dicta, An. Dom. 1674."

It was a duodecimo volume of 156 pages only, licensed and entered at Stationers' Hall, and came out by July 1, 1674.

---

[36] B. M. 1134 a 5 and G 16100.

[37] B. M. E 1958 (19).

[38] B. M. 1083 h 7, and G 3546 with MS. notes.

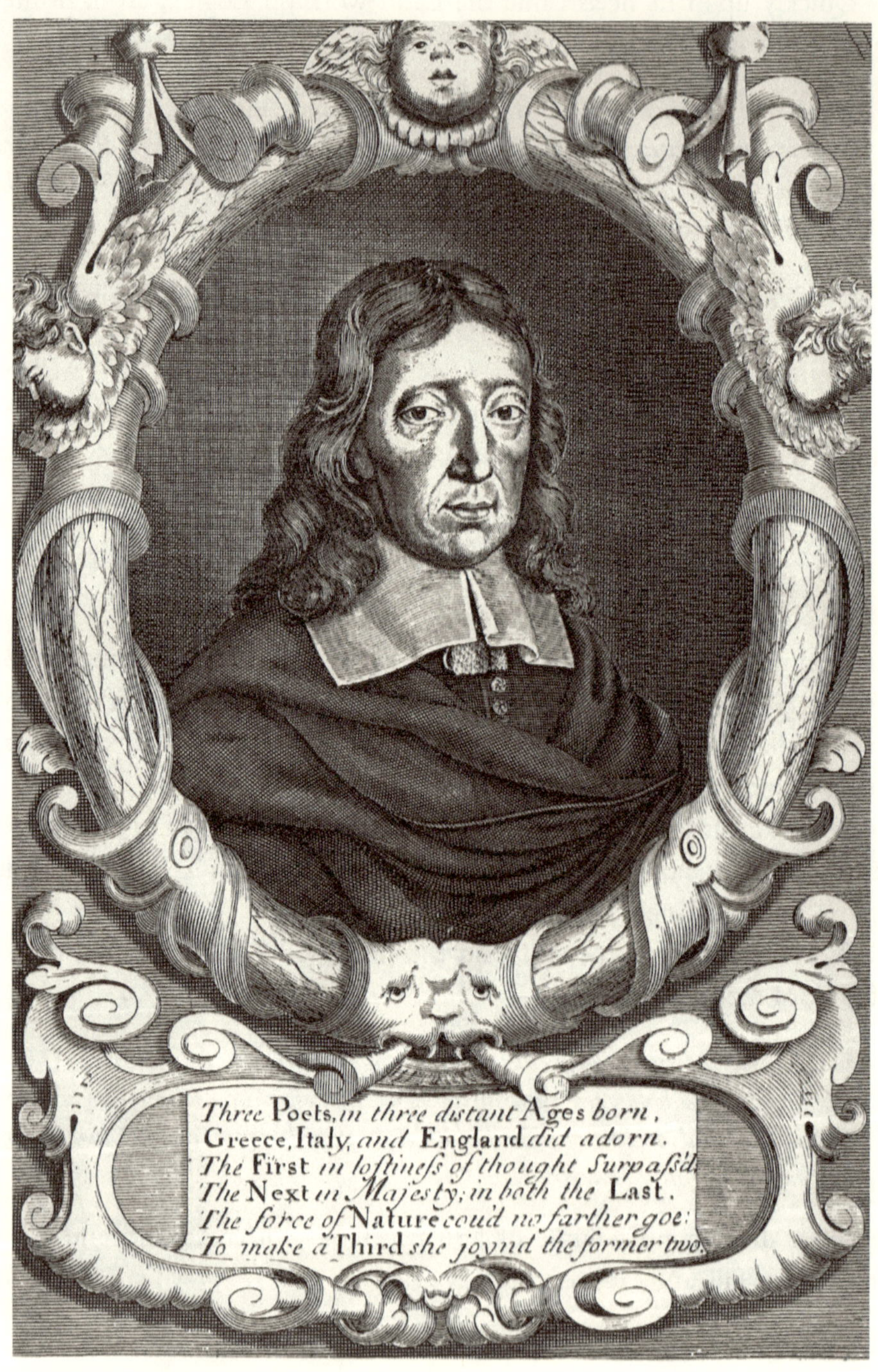

Engraving of John Milton by R. White, forming the Frontispiece to the 4th Edition of *Paradise Lost*, folio, Tonson, 1688. See (31).

Lastly the same friendly bookseller, Brabazon Aylmer, published a small quarto anonymous tract[39] of 12 pages in July 1674 or a little later with this title:—

> "*A Declaration. Or Letters Patents of the Election of this present King of Poland John the Third, Elected on the 22d of May last past, Anno Dom. 1674. Containing the Reasons of this Election, the great Vertues and Merits of the said Serene Elect, His eminent Services in War, especially in his last great Victory against the Turks and Tartars, whereof many Particulars are here related, not published before. Now faithfully translated from the Latin Copy. London, Printed for Brabazon Aylmer, at the Three Pigeons in Cornhill, 1674.*"

but by November of that year Milton had passed away, dying on Sunday November 8th, at his house at Bunhill. He was buried in his own parish church of St. Giles, Cripplegate, on the 12th of the same month. It is possible that he never saw the book on Poland.

In conclusion a few notes as to the chief issues immediately following Milton's death may be of service.

The third edition of Paradise Lost, a small octavo, appeared in 1678, printed by *S. Simmons next door to the Golden Lion in Aldersgate Street*[40]. The second edition[41] of *Paradise Regained* with *Samson Agonistes* came out in 1680, and in that year Simmons sold the copyright of *Paradise Lost* to Brabazon Aylmer, already mentioned, from whom half of it was bought in 1683 by Jacob Tonson.

The folio edition of the Poems came out under Tonson in 1688[42], a fine stately book with R. White's portrait and twelve illustrations by Medina. It was called:—

> "*Paradise Lost. A Poem in Twelve Books. The Authour John Milton. The Fourth Edition, Adorn'd with sculptures. London, Printed by Miles Flesher, for Jacob Tonson, at the Judge's Head in Chancery lane near Fleet-street. MDCLXXXVIII.*"

In the same size and type appeared a third edition[43] of *Paradise Regained* and *Samson Agonistes*, printed by Randal Taylor, whose name appears thus in the

---

[39] B. M. E 1959 (3).

[40] B. M. 11626 b 29.

[41] B. M. 11626 b 30.

[42] B. M. 11607 k 6.

[43] B. M. 11607 k 6 (2).

imprint:—"printed by R. E., and are to be sold by Randal Taylor near Stationers'-Hall."

In some copies of the folio of *Paradise Lost*, Tonson is declared as being in conjunction with a joint holder of copyright, *Richard Bently at the Post Office in Russell Street* and he probably held Aylmer's other half of the copyright, but soon Tonson acquired this also, and the next issue, the fifth, which came out in 1692 in folio, bound up with a fourth of *Paradise Regained*, was Tonson's own property.

In 1695 there was a sixth edition, also in folio, and a uniform issue of *Paradise Regained*, *Samson Agonistes* and the Minor Poems, and in 1705 came an edition of the Poetical Works in 2 vols. large octavo, one in 2 vols. smaller octavo in 1707, a pocket duodecimo edition of *Paradise Lost* in 1711, and an issue of the other poems to match in 1713.

The Tonsons also issued Tickell's edition of the Poems in 2 vols. quarto in 1720, a duodecimo edition in 1721, the Fenton edition in 1725-27 and 30, and Bentley's edition of *Paradise Lost* in 1732.

The Latin State Letters[44] came out in 1676, a neatly printed duodecimo of 234 pages with an anonymous Latin preface, the title being thus:—

"*Literae Pseudo-Senatûs Anglicani, Cromwellii, Religuorumque Perduellium nomine ac jussu conscriptae a Joanne Miltono. Impressae Anno 1676.*"

This was followed by a quarto of 11 pages bearing the title:—

"*Mr. John Milton's Character of the Long Parliament and Assembly of Divines. In MDCXLI. Omitted in his other Works, and never before Printed, And very seasonable for these times. London: Printed for Henry Brome, at the Gun at the West-end of St Paul's, 1681.*"

A posthumous work ascribed to Milton, and not accepted as his own work by all bibliographers.

The *History of Moscovy*[45], a work of undoubted authenticity, followed it. It was called:—

"*A Brief History Of Moscovia and of other less known Countries lying eastward of Russia as far as Cathay. Gather'd from the Writings of several Eye-witnesses. By*

---

[44] B. M. 600 a 15.

[45] B. M. 1049 c 2 (1) and G 7289.

John Milton. London, Printed by M. Flesher, for Brabazon Aylmer at the Three Pigeons against the Royal Exchange, 1682."

and Aylmer's advertisement to it reads:—

"This Book was writ by the authour's own hand, before he lost his sight. And some time before his death dispos'd of it [sic] to be printed. But it being small, the Bookseller try'd to have procured some other suitable Piece of the same Authour's to have joyn'd with it, or else it had been publish'd ere now."

Milton's compilations towards a Latin Dictionary never went further than a manuscript collection of notes, but such as it was, it was used in the Cambridge Dictionary of 1693, the following reference to it appearing in the preface to that work:—"they (the compilers) likewise used a manuscript collection in three large folios, digested into an alphabetical order, made by Mr. John Milton out of all the best and purest Roman authors."

In 1743 appeared in folio form a volume of 180 pages entitled:—

"Original Letters and Papers of State, addressed to Oliver Cromwell; concerning the affairs of Great Britain from the year 1649 to 1658. Found among the Political collections of Mr. John Milton. Now first published from the Originals. By John Nickolls, Jun., member of the Society of Antiquaries, London."

and lastly we would refer to Bishop Sumner's editions of Milton's Latin treatise of Christian Doctrine, which was printed from the manuscript found in 1823 in the State Paper Office by Mr. Robert Lemon, the Deputy Keeper. It was a handsome quarto volume[46] from the Cambridge University Press with the title:—

"Joannis Miltoni Angli De Doctrina Christiana Libri Duo Posthumi."

and in the same year appeared his English Translation[47] of the work, with the title:—

"A Posthumous Treatise on The Christian Doctrine, compiled from the Holy Scriptures alone, in two Books: By John Milton."

---

[46] B. M. 4375 g and in L. P. 7 b 1.

[47] B. M. 1012 e 17.

The foregoing notes are mainly extracted by the kind permission of Messrs Macmillan from their edition in 6 vols., 1880, of Professor Masson's *Life of John Milton*, and the author of the book before his death gave us also his permission to make such extracts as we desired, so far as his ability to give us this right extended; whenever our treatise on the portraits and books of the poet should appear. It has been thought well, with the full permission of the late Professor Masson, our very kind and generous friend, to put the list into this form of ready access in order to give bibliographers the main facts as to the issue of the books in convenient fashion, and also that the errors of Lowndes may be corrected. Some very few details have been added from our own copies of the books and personal study, and from collation with the examples in the British Museum, while, in order to assist students in London, some references to the numbers in the British Museum Catalogue have been given.

An effort has been made to borrow some special copies of works by Milton from the Tangye collection, but without success. The late Sir R. Tangye possessed the copy of the *Defensio* 1651, given by Milton to Charles Vane, brother to Sir Harry Vane, and inscribed in the author's handwriting, "Ch. Vane ex proprio dono Johannis Miltoni Authoris," perhaps one of the last inscriptions written by him before he became blind.

His first edition of the Poems of 1645 belonged to Milton's friend Lord Anglesey, and has his signature in it, and also that of Samuel Pepys. Lord Anglesey gave *2s.* for the book, so he records in it. Sir Richard also owned the Proclamation of Chas. II, 13 Aug. 1660, ordering the burning of two of Milton's books. Mr Green has lent a copy of the first edition of *Paradise Lost*, possessing unusual interest, and a label with full particulars is attached to the book.

G. C. W.

While these pages are passing through the press the earliest portrait of Milton, already alluded to as having been lost sight of for many years, has been re-discovered. It appears to have been sold by Mr. Edgar Disney on 22 March, 1884, and purchased by Mr. J. Passmore-Edwards, who has been good enough to lend it to the exhibition. It was painted in 1618, and is believed to have been one of the very earliest portraits executed in England by the young Dutch painter, Cornelius Janssen, who came over from Amsterdam in that very year and settled in Black Friars, London. It is that of a very grave and intelligent Puritan boy with auburn hair. Its history is exceedingly interesting. Aubrey mentions it as being well known to him, and in his time, in the possession of Milton's widow in London. When Vertue saw Deborah Clarke, the poet's youngest and only surviving daughter, then residing in Spitalfields, in 1721, she told him that her step-mother (or as Vertue calls her in his letter of 12 August,—mother-in-law), living in Cheshire had two portraits of her father, one of which represented him as a school boy. The picture was in the possession of Mrs. Milton at the time of her death in 1727, and is mentioned in the inventory of her effects at Nantwich, the original of which Mr. Marsh reprinted for the Lancashire and Cheshire Historical Society. From the executors of Milton's widow it was bought by Mr. Charles Stanhope for twenty guineas, and at his sale Mr. Thomas Hollis bought it, 3 June, 1760, for thirty-one guineas. As already mentioned on page 5, it passed into the possession of Mr. Thomas Brand Hollis, Dr. Disney and Mr. Edgar Disney, and while in the hands of the last named owner it was seen and described by Professor Masson. As Masson well states "the prevailing expression on the face is a lovable seriousness, and in looking at it one can well imagine that the lines from *Paradise Regained*, which the first engraver ventured to inscribe under the portrait, were written by the poet with some reference to his own recollected childhood." The picture is the one which Lord Harrington, Mr. Stanhope's relative, wished to have returned to him after the sale, and he was told by Mr. Hollis, who had bought it, that "his lordship's whole estate should not re-purchase it." It seemed hardly possible that a portrait of such importance should have disappeared, and it is very satisfactory to know that it is in the possession of an owner who thoroughly values it. It may now be hoped that the missing Onslow portrait may be discovered.

Attention should also be directed to the series of original copper plates purchased by Mr. Shipley while the catalogue was being printed. They are the plates for the Richardson etchings, for the second Faithorne portrait, and for the miniature by Cooper mentioned in the long controversy in the pages of the *Gentleman's Magazine*.

The College is exhibiting also, a pencil sketch of Milton's mulberry tree as it appeared in the beginning of the last century and two photographs of his cottage at Chalfont, while the Treasury, at the desire of the Trustees of the National Portrait Gallery, has been good enough to lend the so-called portrait of the poet by Van der Plas.

G. C. W.

APPENDIX

A Clare College
B Corpus Christi College
C Christ's College
D Downing College
E Emmanuel College
F Fitzwilliam Museum
G Gonville and Caius College
H Trinity Hall
J St John's College
K King's College
L Pembroke College
M Magdalene College
N St Catharine's College
O Jesus College
P Peterhouse
Q Queens' College
R Selwyn College Hostel
S Sidney Sussex College
T Trinity College
U University Library
Y Pepys Library

MILTONIANA

The following list merely contains the titles of Milton's writings or of books relating to Milton, copies of which are to be found in the University of Cambridge, or of books which have been specially lent for this exhibition.

1632

230. Shakespeare. Comedies, etc. Ed. 2.   *Lond.* F°. UT.
      Lent by Trinity College.

1637

231. Comus.   *Lond.* 4°. T.

1638

232. Edwardi King Justa (Lycidas).   *Camb.* 4°. UT.
      Lent by Trinity College.

1640

233. Shakespeare Poems.   *Lond.* 8°. U.
      Lent by the University Library.

1641

234. Of Reformation.   [*Lond.*] 4°. T.
      Lent by Trinity College.
235. Of Prelatical Episcopacy.   *Lond.* 4°. UJT.
      Lent by the University Library.
236. Reason of Church Government.   *Lond.* 4°. T.
      Lent by W. Aldis Wright, Esq.
237. Animadversions against Smectymnuus.   *Lond.* 4°. UT.
238. Short view of the prelatical church.   [*Lond.*] 4°. U.
239.   ”   ”   ” Newly corrected.   *Lond.* 4°. U.

1642

240. Apology for Smectymnuus.   *Lond.* 4°. UT.
      Lent by the University Library.

241. Observations upon His Majesties Answers. (Spurious) *Lond.* 4°. M.
242. Reply to the answer. (Spurious)   *Lond.* 4°. M.
    Lent by Magdalene College.

1643

243. Doctrine and Discipline of Divorce. Ed. 1.   *Lond.* 4°. UGQ.
    Lent by Queens' College.

1644

244. Doctrine and Discipline of Divorce. Ed. 2. State A.
                                                         Lond. 4°. UEQT.
    Lent by J. F. Payne, Esq., M.D.
245. Judgment of M. Bucer concerning Divorce.   *Lond.* 4°. UEQ.
246. Letter to Mr. Hartlib.   *Lond.* 4°. UC.
    Presented by F. H. Cripps-Day, Esq.
247. Areopagitica. Ed. 1.   *Lond.* 4°. UEQT.
    Lent by the University Library.
248. An Answer to the Doctrine and Discipline.   *Lond.* 4°. U.
    Lent by the University Library.

1645

249. Doctrine and Discipline of Divorce. Ed. 2. State B. (no errata).
                                                             Lond. 4°.
    Lent by J. F. Payne, Esq., M.D.
250. Doctrine and Discipline of Divorce. Ed. 2. State C. (two line errata).
                                                           Lond. 4°. U.
251.   „   State D. (three line errata).
                                                           Lond. 4°. T.
252. Tetrachordon.   *Lond.* 4°. UEQT.
    Lent by the University Library.
253. Colasterion.   *Lond.* 4°. UET.
254. Poems English and Latin.   *Lond.* 4°. UCEFT.

1649

255. Defensio Regia pro Carolo I. (Salmasius.)   F°. UM.
    Lent by the University Library.

256. Εἰκονοκλάστης. Ed. 1.   *Lond.* 4°. UET.
       Lent by Trinity College.
257. Tenure of Kings and Magistrates. Ed. A. (Large 'Kings'.)
                                                   Lond. 4°. U.
       Lent by the University Library.
258. Tenure of Kings and Magistrates. Ed. B. (Small 'Kings'.)
                                                   Lond. 4°. U.
       Lent by the University Library.
259. Goodwin (J.). The obstructours of Justice.   *Lond.* 4°. U.
       Lent by the University Library.

1650

260. Εἰκονοκλάστης. Ed. 2.   *Lond.* 4°. UCE.
261. Grand Case of Conscience.   *Lond.* 4°. J.
       Lent by St. John's College.
262. Tenure of Kings and Magistrates.   *Lond.* 4°. UT.

1651

263. Pro populo Anglicano Defensio.   F°. UB.
264.   ”   ”   ”   State A.   4°. (Shaded.) UCL.
265.   ”   ”   ”   State B.   4°. (Plain.) UCO.
266.   ”   ”   ”   *Lond.* 12°. UCEJKOT.
267. C. Salmasii Defensio Regia et J. Miltoni Defensio pro populo.
                                                   Parisiis. 4°. C.

1652

268. Εἰκονοκλάστης ou Réponse au Livre (traduite).   *Lond.* 12°. U.
269. Pro populo Anglicano defensio.   *Lond.* 12°. UAJMLST.
270. Pro rege et populo anglicano apologia.   *Antw.* 12°. E.
271. [A. Mori] Regii Sanguinis clamor.   *Hag. Com.* 12°. UM.

1653

272. An Apology for Smectymnuus, &c. [ab. 1653].   *Lond.* 4°. U.
273. Rowland (J.). Polemica.   [*Antwerp.*] 12°. U.
274. Ziegler (C.). Circa Regicidium Anglorum.   *Lugd. Bat.* 12°. M.

1654

275.	Pro populo Anglicano defensio secunda.	*Lond.* 8°. UCGL.
276.	" " "	*Hag. Com.* 12°. UEOT.
277.	A. Mori Fides Publica.	*Hag. Com.* 12°. UM.

1655

278.	Pro se defensio.	*Lond.* 8°. CE.
279.	" "	*Hag. Com.* 12°. U.
280.	Scriptum Protectoris.	*Lond.* 4°. T.

Lent by Trinity College.

1658

| 281. | Raleigh (Sir W.). The Cabinet Council. | *Lond.* 8°. UM. |

1659

282.	Considerations touching hirelings.	*Lond.* 12°. UCGJ.
283.	Treatise of Civil Power in Ecclesiastical Cases.	*Lond.* 4°. UE.
284.	" " "	*Lond.* 12°. UE.

1660

| 285. | Salmasius (C.). Ad J. Miltonum responsio. | *Divione.* 4°. UM. |

Lent by the University Library.

286.	Salmasius (C.).	*Lond.* 8°. M.
287.	Salmasius His Dissection.	*Lond.* 4°. U.
288.	Proclamation, Aug. 13. State A (with misprint).	*Lond.* Broadside.

Photograph lent by the Rev. J. W. Cartmell.

| 289. | Proclamation, Aug. 13. State B. | *Lond.* Broadside. |

Lent by J. F. Payne, Esq., M.D.

| 290. | Griffith (M.). The Fear of God. | *Lond.* 8°. UM. |

Lent by the University Library.

| 291. | Brief notes upon a late sermon by M. Griffith. | *Lond.* 4°. U. |

Lent by the University Library.

| 292. | The Censure of the Rota. | *Lond.* MT. |
| 293. | L'Estrange (R.). No Blind Guides. | *Lond.* 4°. ULM. |

Lent by the University Library.

| 294. | Way to a Free Commonwealth. Ed. 1. | *Lond.* 4°. U. |

294.   Way to a Free Commonwealth. Ed. 1.   *Lond.* 4°. U.
          Lent by J. F. Payne, Esq., M.D.
295.   Way to a Free Commonwealth. Ed. 2.   *Lond.* 12°.
          Lent by J. F. Payne, Esq., M.D.

1665

296.   Warrant against Thomas Ellwood.
          Photograph of the original MS.
          Lent by the Rev. J. W. Cartmell.

1667

297.   Paradise Lost. [No. 1.]   *Lond.* 4°. CT.
298.   ”   ”   [No. 2.]   *Lond.* 4°. C.

1668

299.   P. L. [No. 3.]   4°. T.
300.   P. L. [No. 4.]   4°. UC.
        P. L. [Nos. 5, 6 not known.]   4°.

1669

301.   P. L. [No. 7.]   CT.
302.   P. L. [No. 8.]   UCJMPT.
303.   Accedence.   *Lond.* 12°. CT.

1670

304.   History of Britain.   *Lond.* 4°. UEG.

1671

305.   P. R. and S. A. Ed. 1.   *Lond.* 8°. UCMT.
306.   History of Britain.   4°. UJT.

1672

307.   Artis logicae plenior institutio.   *Lond.* 12°. UAEMT.
          Lent by the University Library.

1673

308. Poems, &c.   *T. Dring at the Blew Anchor.* 8°. UT.
      Lent by the University Library.
309. Poems, &c.   *T. Dring at the White Lion. Lond.* 8°. L.
      Lent by Pembroke College.
310. Artis logicae plenior Institutio.   *Lond.* 12°. C.

1674

311. P. L. Ed. 2.   *Lond.* 8°. CFT.
312. Epistolarum liber unus.   *Lond.* 12°. CKLQ.

1676

313. Literae pseudo-senatus.   [*Lond.*] 12°. UACJKORT.

1677

314. History of Britain.   *Lond.* 8°. UCJQT.

1678

315. P. L. Ed. 3.   *Lond.* 8°. UCJT.

1679

316. Filmer (Sir R.). The Freeholder's Grand Inquest.   *Lond.* 8°. U.

1680

317. P. R. and Samson Agonistes.   *Lond.* 8°. U.

1681

318. Character of the Long Parliament.   *Lond.* 4°. UEJQ.

1682

319. Brief History of Moscovia.   *Lond.* 12°. UJ.

1684

320. Mackenzie (Sir G.). Jus Regium.   *Lond.* 8°. U.

1688

321. P. L. Ed. 4. With sculptures. State A.

M. Flesher for J. Tonson, Lond. F°. UCPTY.

322. P. L. Ed. 4. With sculptures. State B.

M. Flesher for R. Bentley. F°. GJ.

323. P. R. and S. A.   *Lond.* F°. UCO.

1690

324. Εἰκονοκλάστης.   *Amst.* 8°. UACQT.
325. Hogaeus (Gul.). Paraphrasis poetica.   *Lond.* 8°. UEJQL.

1691

326. P. L. Ed. 5. First issue.   *Lond.* F°. T.
     Lent by Trinity College.
327. P. L. Bk. 1. (Lat.).   *Cantab.* 4°. GQ.

1692

328. P. L. Ed. 5. Second issue.   *Lond.* F°. OQ.
329. Defence of the People of England.   *Lond.* 8°. CE.
330. Vindiciae Carolinae.   *Lond.* 8°. T.
     Lent by Trinity College.

1694

331. Letters of State. Ed. E. Phillips.   *Lond.* 12°. UCEJTY.

1695

332. Poetical Works with notes by P. H[ume] and Sculptures. (P. L. Ed.
     6. P. R. and S. A. Poems. Ed. 3.)

J. Tonson. Lond. F°. UAHTL.

     Lent by Pembroke College.

1697

333. Prose Works.   [*Lond.*] F°. J.
     Lent by H. Rackham, Esq.

1698

334.   Complete Historical, Political and Miscellaneous Works. 3 vols.
                                  'Amst.' [*Lond.*] F°. UBKJYCLN.

335.   Comœdia J. Miltoni paraphrastice reddita.   *Lond.* 4°. Q.

1699

336.   Amyntor; or a defence of Milton's Life.   *Lond.* 8°. UGY.
337.   Life [by J. Toland].   *Lond.* 8°. UJ.
      Lent by St John's College.
338.   Remarks on the Life of Milton as published by H. T.
                                            Lond. 8°. T.
339.   Some reflections on Amyntor. [By S. Clarke]   *Lond.* 8°. U.

1705

340.   P. L. Ed. 7. (P. R., S. A. and Poems. Ed. 4.)   *Lond.* 8°. UGJT.

1706

341.   History of Britain.   *Lond.* F°. P.

1707

342.   P. L. Ed. 8.   *Lond.* 8°. ET.
      Lent by Trinity College.

1709

343.   Milton's sublimity asserted by Philo Milton.   *Lond.* 8°. T.

1710

344.   Satire against Hypocrites.   *Lond.* 8°. T.
      Lent by Trinity College.

1711

345.   P. L. Ed. 9. With sculptures.   *Lond.* 12°. CLT.

1713

346.   P. R. Ed. 5.   *Lond.* 12°. UT.

1715

| 347. | P. R. and S. A. | *Lond.* F°. L. |

1719

348. P. L. Ed. 10. With sculptures.   *Lond.* 12°. ET.
    Lent by Trinity College.
349. Notes upon P. L. by J. Addison.   *Lond.* 12°. J.
    Lent by St John's College.

1720

350. P. W. 2 vols.   *Lond.* 4°. JT.
    Lent by Trinity College.

1725

351. P. L. Ed. 12.   *Lond.* 8°. ST.
    Lent by Sidney Sussex College.
352. P. R. Ed. 6.   *Lond.* 8°. ST.

1727

353. P. L. Ed. 13.   *Lond.* 8°. T.
    Lent by Trinity College.
354. P. R. Ed. 7.   *Lond.* 8°. T.

1730

355. P. L. Ed. 14.   *Lond.* 12°. T.
    Lent by Trinity College.

1732

356. P. L. Ed. R. Bentley.   *Lond.* 4°. UJGTLSR.
    With the autograph signature of William Cowper and notes by W. Hayley.
    Presented by J. W. Clark, Esq.
357. Dr. Bentley's emendations on P. L.   *Lond.* 12°.
    Lent by J. W. Clark, Esq.
358. Review of...Bentley. Pts 1 and 2. [By Z. Pearce.]   *Lond.* 8°. UJ.
    Lent by St John's College.

142

359. A Friendly letter to Dr. Bentley on P. L. Ed. 1.   *Lond.* 8°.
          Lent by J. W. Clark, Esq.
360. Milton restor'd and Bentley depos'd. No. 1.   *Lond.* 8°. T.
          Lent by Trinity College.

1733

361. Review of Bentley. Pt 3. [By Z. Pearce.]   *Lond.* 8°. Q.

1734

362. Richardson (J.). Explanatory Notes. 2 vols.   *Lond.* 8°. QT.

1736

363. Paradiso Perduto. Trad. P. Rolli.   *Lond.* F°. UF.

1738

364. Complete Historical Works. Ed. T. Birch. 2 vols.
                              A. Millar, Lond. F°. CHJOPT.
365. P. L. Ed. 15.   T.
          Lent by Trinity College.
366. Comus: adapted for the stage. Ed. 1.   *Lond.* 8°. T.
          Lent by Trinity College.
367. Comus: adapted for the stage. Ed. 2.   *Lond.* 8°. U.
368.   ”   ”   ”   *Dublin.* 8°. JL.
369. Arne (T. A.). Musick of Comus.   *Lond.* 4°.
          Lent by E. J. Dent, Esq.

1740

370. Handel. L'Allegro. (MS. Study.)   F.
371. New Memoirs by F. Peck.   *Lond.* 4°. UBJT.

1741

372. Handel. Samson. (MS. fragment.)   F.
373. Verbal Index to P. L. [By H. J. Todd.]   [*Lond.*] 12°. UT.
374. Essay upon Milton's Imitations.   *Lond.* 8°. T.
          Lent by Trinity College.

1743

375. P. R. and S. A.   *Lond.* 8°. L.
      Lent by Pembroke College.
376. Considerations touching Hirelings. Ed. 3.   *Lond.* T.
377. Samson (Libretto).   *Lond.* 8°.
      Lent by Dr. A. H. Mann.

1744

378. Paterson (J.). Complete commentary on P. L.   *Lond.* 12°. U.
      Lent by the University Library.

1747

379. P. L. Ed. J. Hawkey.   *Dublin.* 8°. U.
380. Richardson (R.). Zoilomastix.   *Lond.* 8°. U.

1748

381. Meadowcourt (R.). Critical Dissertation on P. R. Ed. 2.
                                                                   Lond. 8°. UQ.

      Lent by the University Library.

1749

382. P. L. Ed. T. Newton. Ed. 1. 2 vols.   *Lond.* 4°. UCNOT.

1750

383. P. L. Ed. T. Newton. Ed. 2. 2 vols.   *Lond.* 8°. Q.
384. P. L. Book I.   *Glasgow.* 8°. U.
385. Paradisus amissus. (Lat) G. Dobson.   *Oxon.* 4°. UJL.
386. Comus. Adapted to the Stage.   *Lond.* 8°. T.
387. An Essay of Milton's use of the Moderns.   *Lond.* 8°. UF.

1751

388. Essay on Education.   *Lond.* 8°. T.
389. Douglas (John). Milton vindicated.   *Lond.* 8°. Q.

144

1752

390.	P. L.	*Glasgow.* 12°. Q.
391.	P. R. Ed. T. Newton.	*Lond.* 4°. UCFNOPT.
392.	P. R. Ed. J. Hawkey.	*Dublin.* 8°. U.
393.	Lauder (W.). Delectus auctorum. 2 vols.	*Lond.* 8°. UK.

1753

394.	Works Hist., Pol. and Misc. Ed. T. Birch. 2 vols.	
		Lond. 4°. UACFKNQ.
395.	P. L. (Lat.) G. Dobson.	*Oxon.* 4°. J.
396.	Tractate of Education to S. Hartlib.	*Berwick.* 8°. T.

1754

397.	P. L. Ed. Newton. 2 vols.	*Lond.* 4°. CP.

1757

398.	P. L. Ed. T. Newton. Ed. 4. 2 vols.	*Lond.* 8°. L.

1758

399.	P. L. State A.	*Baskerville.* 8°. UBH.
400.	State B.	” 8°. KQ.
401.	P. R.	” 8°. UBHK.
402.	Samson. An Oratorio adapted.	*Lond.* 4°. T.

1759

403.	P. L. State A.	*Baskerville.* 4°. C.
404.	State B.	” 4°. FK.
405.	P. R.	” 4°. CFKQ.

1760

406.	P. L.	” 8°. U.
407.	P. R.	” 8°. U.
408.	P. R. and S. A. Ed. T. Newton. Ed. 3. 2 vols.	*Lond.* 8°. LR.
409.	P. L.	*Lond.* 12°. UF.
410.	Comus. Altered for the Stage.	*Lond.* 8°. U.

145

1761

411.   Poetical Works. Ed. T. Newton. 3 vols.   *Lond.* 4°. K.

1762

412.   A familiar explanation of Milton. With Addison's criticism and
  preface by Dodd.

Lond. 12°. UJ.

1766

413.   L'Allegro et le Pensieroso. Trad. en vers françois.   *Lond.* 4°. U.

1770

414.   P. L.   *Glasgow.* F°. H.
  Lent by Trinity Hall.
415.   P. L. Bk. I. Gr. [T. Stratford], Lat. G. Dobson.   *Dublin.* 4°. U.

1772

416.   P. R. and S. A.   *Lond.* 12°. QT.

1773

417.   P. W. Ed. T. Newton. 4 vols.   *Lond.* 8°. G.

1774

418.   P. L. An Oratorio. Set to music by Mr. Smith.   *Lond.* 4°. T.
419.   Comus, altered as performed at Covent Garden.   *Lond.* 8°. T.

1775

420.   P. L. Ed. T. Newton. Ed. 8. 2 vols.   *Lond.* 4°. UFA.

1777

421.   P. R. Ed. T. Newton.   *Lond.* 4°. AC.

1778

422.   P. L. Ed. T. Newton. Ed. 8. 2 vols.   *Lond.* 8°. T.

1780

423. Remarks on Johnson's Life of Milton, with Milton's Tractate on Education and Areopagitica. [By F. Blackburne.]
Lond. 12°. UT.

1782

424. Samson. [Libretto.] Handel.
F. Hodson and Wynne Cambridge. 8°. T.
Lent by Trinity College.
425. L'Allegro and Il Penseroso. [Libretto.]
F. Hodson and Wynne Cambridge. 8°. T.

1783

426. P. W. 3 vols. *Lond* [*Lyons*]. 12°.
Lent by E. Ph. Goldschmidt, Esq.

1785

427. P. R. Ed. T. Newton. 2 vols. *Lond.* 8°. T.
428. Minor Poems. Ed. T. Warton. Ed. 1. *Lond.* 8°. KT.
429. L'Allegro (Domenico Testa). *Parma.* 4°. U.

1787

430. Comus. At the Theatre Royal, Covent Garden. *Lond.* 12°. U.
431. Comus. At the Theatres Royal. *Lond.* 12°. U.
Lent by the University Library.

1788

432. P. L. Ill. J. Gillies. Ed. 1. *Lond.* 12°. U.
433. Samson Agonistes. *Oxon.* 8°. K.

1790

434. Treatise of civil power. *Lond.* 8°. UK.
435. Narrative of the disinterment of Milton's coffin. [By Ph. Neve.] Ed. 2. *Lond.* 4°.
Lent by J. F. Payne, Esq., M.D.

147

1791

436. Poems upon several occasions. Ed. T. Warton. Ed. 2.
      Lond. 8°. UFGP.
437. Comus adapted.   *Lond.* 12°. T.
    Lent by Trinity College.

1792

438. P. L. Books I-IV. Ill. Stothard and Bartolozzi.   *Lond.* F°. UKP.
    Lent by Peterhouse.

1793

439. P. L. Ill. J. Gillies. Ed. 2.   *Lond.* 12°. U.
440. P. W. (Anderson, Vol. v.)   *Edinburgh.* 8°. U.

1794

441. Poetical Works, with life by W. Hayley. 3 vols.
      Bulmer, Lond. F°. UEF.
442. P. L. Ill. J. and H. Richter.   *Lond.* 4°. U.
443. Il Paradiso Perduto. Trad. F. Mariottini. Vol. 1.   *Lond.* 8°. U.

1796

444. Hayley (W.). Life of Milton.   *Lond.* 4°. U.
445. S. A.   *Lond.* 12°. T.

1797

446. Lycidas, Graecé redditum. J. Plumptre.   [*Lond.*] 4°. UKT.

1798

447. Comus. Ed. H. J. Todd.   *Canterbury.* 8°. UT.

1800

448. P. R. Ed. C. Dunster.   *Lond.* 4°. T.
    Lent by Trinity College.
449. Dunster (C.). Considerations on Milton's early reading.
      Lond. 8°. U.

1801

450. P. W. Ed. Todd (Ed. 3). 6 vols.   *Lond.* 8°. FJT.

1805

451. Mortimer (C. E.). Memoir.   *Lond.* 4°. U.

1806

452. P. W. Preface S. Johnson. Ed. J. Aikin. 3 vols.   *Lond.* 8°. J.
453. Prose Works. Ed. C. Symmons. 7 vols.   *Lond.* 8°. UFRT.

1808

454. Latin and Italian Poems. Trans. W. Cowper. With Flaxman's
      illustrations.

Chichester. 4°. U.

Lent by the University Library.

1809

455. P. W. Ed. H. J. Todd. Ed. 2. 7 vols.   *Lond.* 8°. UCEHJPT.
456. Todd (H. J.). Some account of the Life. Ed. 2.   *Lond.* 8°. C.

1810

457. Symmons (C.). Life. Ed. 2.   *Lond.* 8°. E.

1811

458. Il Paradiso Perduto. Trad. L. Papi. 3 vols.   *Lucca.* 8°. U.

1812

459. Licida. Trad. T. J. Mathias.   *Londra.* 8°. ULT.

1813

460. P. L.   *Lond.* 12°. C.

1815

461. Reflections on the Civil War.   *Lond.* 8°. U.
462. Goodwin (W.). Lives. [J. Aubrey, E. Phillips]   *Lond.* 4°. U.

149

463. Bishop (Sir H. R.). Music to Comus.   *Lond.* 4°.
      Lent by J. E. Nixon, Esq.

1816

464. P. R. etc. (Engraved title only.)   *Lond.* 12°.
      Lent by O. Johnson, Esq.

1817

465. P. L. 2 vols.   *Lond.* 8°. R.
466. Il Paradiso Perduto. Rec. M. Leoni.   *Pisa.* 8°. U.

1819

467. Coll gwyfa. W. O. Pughe.   *Llundain.* 8°. U.
468. Areopagitica. Ed. T. Holt White. With tract by Mirabeau.
                                                          Lond. 8°. UB.

1820

469. Milton's plan of education in his letter to Hartlib (Pamphleteer).
                                                           Lond. 8°. U.

1822

470. Poems. 3 vols.   *Chiswick.* 8°. L.
471. Vindication of P. L., by Philo-milton.   8°. U.
472. Siddons (S.). Story of our first parents.   *Lond.* 8°. U.

1823

473. P. R. etc.   *Lond.* 12°.
      Lent by O. Johnson, Esq.

1825

474. De Doctrina Christiana. Ed. C. R. Sumner.
                                                 Cantab. 4°. UCKOPQT.
475. Treatise on Christian Doctrine. Trans. C. R. Sumner.
                                                   Lond. 4°. UCKOPQT.
476. Channing (W. E). Remarks.   *Lond.* 8°. U.

1826

477. Poetical Works. Ed. H. J. Todd.   *Lond.* 8°. K.
478. Todd (H. J.). Some account of the Life.   *Lond.* 8°. U.
479. Burgess (T.). Protestant Union. With preface on Milton.
      Lond. 8°. U.

1827

480. The poetry of Milton's prose.   *Lond.* 8°. U.

1828

481. P. L.   *Pickering, Lond.* 24°.
    Lent by Professor T. McK. Hughes.
482. Paradiser Missir a Islensku. Joni Thortakssyni.
      8°. *Kaupmannahöfn.* UKT.
483. Cann (C.). Glossary to Paradise Lost.   *Lond.* 8°. U.
484. Channing (W. E.). Remarks.   *Lond.* 8°. U.
485. Last Thoughts on the Trinity, extracted from a Treatise of
    Christian Doctrine.
      Lond. 8°. L.

1832

486. Fabulae Samson et Comus graecé interpr. E. Greswell.
      Oxon. 8°. LRT.

1833

487. Ivimey (J.). John Milton.   *Lond.* 8°. U.
488. Prose Works. Ed. R. Fletcher.   *Lond.* 8°. L.

1834-5

489. Prose Works. Ed. R. Fletcher.   8°. UC.

1835

490. P. W. Ed. Sir E. Brydges. Ill. J. M. W. Turner. 6 vols.   8°. U.
    Lent by the University Library.
491. P. L. Bks I-IV. Ed. J. R. Major.   8°. U.

492. P. L.   *Pickering, Lond.* 24°.
      Lent by Professor T. McK. Hughes.

1836

493. Select Prose Works. Ed. J. A. St John. 2 vols.   *Lond.* 8°. U.
494. Le Paradis Perdu. Trad. Chateaubriand. 2 tom.   *Paris.* 8°. U.
495. Extracts from the Prose Works.   *Edinburgh.* 8°. L.

1838

496. Areopagitica Secunda on Talfourd's Bill.   *Lond.* 8°. T.

1839

497. Treatise of Civil Power. (Tracts for the People.)   *Lond.* 12°. U.

1840

498. P. L. Ed. J. Prendeville.   8°. U.
499. Areopagitica.   *Lond.* 12°. U.

1843

500. P. W. Ed. J. Montgomery. 2 vols.   8°. U.

1846

501. P. L. Poem in twelv bucs.   *Lundun.* 8°. U.

1848

502. Prose Works. Ed. J. A. St John. 5 vols.   *Bohn. Lond.* 8°. UK.
503. Geoffroy (A.). Étude sur les pamphlets.   *Paris.* 8°. U.

1849

504. L'Allegro. Ill. by the Etching Club.   *Lond.* 4°. U.

1851

505. Works. Ed. J. Mitford. 8 vols.   *Pickering, Lond.* 8°. UCT.
506. P. L. Ed. J. J. Flatters.   F°. U.
507. Papers. Ed. by J. F. Marsh.   *Manchester.* 4°. UT.

1852

508. Hood (E. P.). John Milton.   *Lond.* 12°. U.

1853

509. P. W. Illustrated.   *T. Nelson, Lond.* 8°. U.
     Lent by Dr. J. E. Sandys.
510. P. W. Ed. G. Gilfillan.   *Edin.* 8°. U.
511. P. L. With notes by J. R. Major.   *Lond.* 12°. U.
512. P. L. Ed. T. Thomson.   *Lond.* 8°. U.

1855

513. P. L. Books I-IV. Ed. C. W. Connon.   8°. U.
514. L'Allegro and Il Penseroso. Ill. B. Foster.   *Lond.* F°. U.
     Lent by G. L. Keynes, Esq.
515. Life by T. Keightley.   *Lond.* 8°. UT.

1857

516. P. L. and P. R. Ed. J. Edmonston.   *Lond.* 8°. L.
517. P. L. Selections. Ed. R. Demaus.   *Edin.* 8°. U.
518. Complete Concordance by G. L. Prendergast.   *Madras.* 4°. UT.

1858

519. P. W. Ed. T. Newton.   *Lond.* 8°. G.
520. Comus. Illustrated by Pickersgill, etc.   *Lond.* 8°. U.
     Lent by the University Library.

1859

521. P. W. Ed. T. Keightley. 2 vols.   UT.
522. L'Allegro.   *Lond.* 8°. U.
523. Original Papers. Ed. W. D. Hamilton. (Camden Society.)
                                              Lond. 4°. UJK.
524. Life by D. Masson. Vol. 1.   *Lond. and Camb.* 8°. UENRT.

1860

525. Comus.   *n. d. Lond.* 8°. U.

153

1861

526. P. L. Book 1. Ed. J. Hunter. Ed. 2.   *Lond.* 8°. U.
527. Sotheby (S. L.). Ramblings.   4°. UCK.
528. Milton's prophecy of Essays and Reviews.   *Lond.* 8°. U.
529. Tulloch (J.). English Puritanism.   *Edinburgh.* 8°. U.

1862

530. P. W. Ill. J. M. W. Turner.   *Lond.* 12°. U.
531. P. L. With Channing's Essay.   *Lond.* 8°. U.
532. Prose Selections. Ed. S. Manning.   *Lond.* 8°. U.
533. P. L. Book II. Ed. J. Hunter.   *Lond.* 8°. U.
534. Morris (J. W.). A vindication from Arianism.   *Lond.* 12°. U.
535. Calverley (C. S.). Verses and Translations.   *Camb.* 8°.
        Lent by the Master of Christ's College.

1863

536. Comus. Graecé redd. G. Baro Lyttelton.

Camb. and Lond. 8°. UC.

1864

537. Comus, L'Allegro, &c.   *Lond.* 8°. U.

1865

538. P. W. and Index. Ed. C. D. Cleveland.   *Lond.* 8°.
        Lent by Professor Skeat.
539. Comus. Graecé. Redd. G. Baro Lyttelton.   *Cantab.* 12°. U.

1866

540. P. W. 3 vols. (Aldine Edition.)   *Lond.* 8°. UN.
541. P. L. Ill. G. Doré.   F°. U.

1867

542. Samson Agonistes. Graece. G. Baro Lyttelton.   *Lond.* 12°. U.
543. Concordance. By C. D. Cleveland.   *Lond.* 8°. UJ.

154

544.	Ode. Illustrated.	*Lond.* 8°. U.
545.	Areopagitica. Ed. Arber.	*Lond.* 8°. HJT.

1869

546.	S. A.	*SPCK, Lond.* 8°. U.
547.	Tomlinson (J). Three household poets.	*Lond.* 12°. U.
548.	Areopagitica. Ed. Arber.	*Lond.* 8°. K.

1870

549.	English Poems. Ed. R. C. Browne. 2 vols.	*Oxford.* 8°. C.
550.	S. A. and Lycidas. Ed. J. Hunter.	*Lond.* 8°. U.
551.	History of Britain (Murray).	*Lond.* 8°. UJ.
552.	Prose Selections. Ed. J. J. G. Graham.	*Lond.* 8°. U.

1871

553.	Poems. Ed. J. M. Ross.	*Lond.* 8°. U.
554.	P. L. in Hebrew. Trans. I. E. Salkinson.	*Wien.* 8°. U.
555.	P. L. Book II. Ed. C. P. Mason. Ed. 2.	*Lond.* 8°. U.
556.	Coll gwnfa. Ed. J. Evans.	*Wrexham.* 8°. U.
557.	Comus, &c. Ed. H. R. Huckin.	*Lond.* 8°. U.
558.	Comus. With Notes. Ed. W. Wallace. (Chamber's English Classics.) *Edinburgh.* 8°. U.	
559.	Masson (D.). Life and History. Vol. 2.	*Lond.* 8°. UCK.

1872

560.	P. W. Ed. W. M. Rossetti.	*Lond.* 8°. U.
561.	P. L. Book III. Ed. J. Hunter.	*Lond.* 8°. U.
562.	P. L. Selections in Manx. Ed. T. Christian.	*Douglas.* 8°. U.
563.	S. A. Ed. A. J. Church.	*Lond.* 8°. U.
564.	Areopagitica. Comm. by R. C. Jebb.	*[Camb.]* 8°. UT.
565.	Autobiography. Ed. J. J. G. Graham.	*Lond.* 8°. U.

1873

566.	P. W. A. Chalmers.	8°. U.

567. P. W. (Chandos Classics.)   *Lond.* 8°. U.
568. P. L.   *B. M. Pickering, Lond.* 8°.
          Lent by Oscar Browning, Esq.
569. P. L. Book III. Ed. C. P. Mason. Ed. 2.   *Lond.* 8°. U.
570. P. L. Books IV, V. Ed. J. Hunter.   *Lond.* 8°. U.
571. Areopagitica. Ed. T. G. Osborn.   *Lond.* 8°. U.
572. Masson (D.). Life. Vol. 3.   *Lond.* 8°. UC.

1874

573. P. W. Ed. Masson. 3 vols.   *Lond.* 8°. UCKNRT.
574. P. L. Books I, II. Ed. F. Storr.   *Lond.* 8°. U.
575. P. L. Books I, II, Comus, Lycidas, etc. Ed. J. G. Davis.   *Lond.* 8°. U.
576. Lycidas and Epitaphium Damonis. Ed. C. S. Jerram.
                                                                  Lond. 8°. UC.
577.   ”   With Latin Hexameter, trans. by F. A. Paley.
                                                                  Lond. 12°. UT.
578. L’Allegro and Il Penseroso. Trans. into French by J. Roberts.
                                                                   Lond. 8°. U.
579. Comus.   *Lond.* 8°. U.
580. Areopagitica. Ed. J. W. Hales.   *Oxford.* 8°. UCR.

1875

581. Comus, L’Allegro, etc. Ed. J. Hunter.   *Lond.* 8°. U.

1876

582. S. A. Ed. J. P. Fleming.   *Lond.* 8°. U.
583. Lycidas. Ed. F. Main. Ed. 1.   *Lond.* 8°. U.
584.   ”   ”   Ed. 2.   *Lond.* 8°. U.
585. L’Allegro. Ed. E. T. Stevens and D. Morris.   *Lond.* 8°. U.
586. Il Penseroso. Ed. E. T. Stevens and D. Morris.   *Lond.* 8°. U.
587. Common Place Book. Ed. A. J. Horwood (Camden Society).
                                                                  Lond. 4°. UKT.
588.   ”   ”   (Privately printed.)   *Lond.* 4°. U.
589. Blake (W.). Illustrations of Comus.   *Manchester.* F°.
          Lent by G. L. Keynes, Esq.

1877

590.	P. W. (Globe.)	*Lond.* 8°. U.
591.	P. L. Facsimile.	4°. U.
592.	P. R. Ed. C. S. Jerram.	*Lond.* 8°. U.
593.	L'Allegro. Ed. F. Main. Ed. 2.	*Lond.* 8°. U.
594.	” Ed. L. Evans.	*Lond.* 8°. U.
595.	Lycidas. Ed. E. T. Stevens and D. Morris.	*Lond.* 8°. U.
596.	” Ed. T. D. Hall.	*Manchester.* 8°. U.
597.	Common Place Book. Ed. A. J. Harwood. Revised.	*Westminster.* 4°. UK.
598.	Masson (D.). Life. Vols. 4 and 5.	*Lond.* 8°. UCJ.
599.	Stein (A.). Milton in seine Zeit.	*Leipzig.* 8°. U.

1878

600.	P. W. Ed. J. Bradshaw.	U.
601.	L'Allegro. Ed. E. Storr.	*Lond.* 8°. U.
602.	Il Penseroso, graece. Redd. F. E. Gretton.	*Camb.* 8°. T.
603.	Britain under Trojan, Roman and Saxon Rule.	*Lond.* 8°. U.

1879

604.	L'Allegro, Il Penseroso and Lycidas. Ed. F. S. Aldhous.	*Dublin.* 8°. U.
605.	Pattison (M.). Milton.	*Lond.* 8°. U.
606.	Thrupp (F.). Paradise Lost.	*Lond.* Obl. F°. U.

1880

607.	P. L. Ed. E. F. Willoughby.	*Lond.* 8°. U.
608.	Arcades and Sonnets. Ed. J. Hunter.	*Lond.* 8°. U.
609.	Masson (D.). Life. Vol. 6.	*Lond.* 8°. UCJ.

1881

610.	P. W. A. Chalmers.	8°. U.
611.	P. W.	*Edinburgh.* 8°. U.
612.	Lycidas and Epitaphium Damonis. Ed. C. S. Jerram. Ed. 2.	*Lond.* 8°. U.
613.	Masson (D.). Life. New ed. Vol. 1.	*Lond.* 8°. UJ.

1882

| 614. | P. W. Ed. W. M. Rossetti. | *Lond.* 8°. U. |
| 615. | P. L. Ill. G. Doré. Ed. R. Vaughan. | *Lond.* 8°. U. |

1883

616.	S. A. Ed. J. C. Collins.	*Oxford.* 8°. U.
617.	Sonnets. Ed. M. Pattison.	*Lond.* 8°. U.
618.	Tractate on Education. Ed. O. Browning.	*Camb.* 8°. UE.

1884

| 619. | P. L. Books I-VI. Ed. M. Mull. | 8°. U. |
| 620. | Selected Prose. Ed. E. Myers. | *Lond.* 8°. U. |

1885

621.	P. W. Ed. J. Bradshaw. Ed. 2.	8°. U.
622.	L'Allegro and Il Penseroso and Hymn.	*Lond.* 8°. U.
623.	Edmundson (G.). Milton and Vondel.	*Lond.* 8°. U.

1886

| 624. | P. R., S. A. and Minor Poems. (R. T. S. Library.) | *Lond.* 8°. U. |
| 625. | Earlier Poems and trans. by W. Cowper. | *Lond.* 8°. U. |

1887

626.	P. W. Vol. 1. Ed. J. Bradshaw. (Canterbury Poets.)	*Lond.* 8°. U.
627.	P. L. Books I and II. Ed. M. Macmillan.	*Lond.* 8°. U.
628.	P. L. Book I. Ed. H. C. Beeching.	*Oxford.* 8°. U.
629.	Willis (William). John Milton: a lecture.	*Lond.* 8°. U.
630.	Birthday Book.	*Lond.* 8°. U.
631.	Parry (C. H. H.). MS. Score of The Blest Pair of Sirens. Lent by Trinity College.	

1888

632.	P. W. Vol. II. Ed. J. Bradshaw. (Canterbury Poets.)	*Lond.* 8°. U.
633.	P. L. Book VII. Ed. L. J. Woodroffe.	*Dublin.* 8°. U.
634.	Comus. Ed. A. M. Williams.	*Lond.* 8°. U.

158

| 635. | Areopagitica, etc. (Cassell.) | *Lond.* 8°. U. |

1889

636.	P. L. and P. R., etc. (Cassell's National Library.)	*Lond.* 8°. U.
637.	L'Allegro, etc. Ed. W. Bell.	*Lond.* 8°. U.
638.	Shorter Poems. Ill. S. Palmer.	4°. U.
639.	English Prose Writings. Ed. H. Morley.	*Lond.* 8°. U.
640.	Newman (Robert). J. Milton: a lecture.	*Lond.* 8°. U.
641.	On the Prosody of P. L. and S. A. [By R. Bridges.]	*Oxford.* 8°. U.

1890

642.	P. W. Ed. Masson. 3 vols.	8°. UG.
643.	S. A. Ed. H. M. Percival.	*Lond.* 8°. U.
644.	S. A. Ed. C. S. Jerram.	*Lond.* 8°. U.
645.	S. A. Ed. A. J. Wyatt.	*Lond.* 8°. U.
646.	S. A. Trans. into Hebrew by J. Massel.	*Manchester.* 8°. U.
647.	Comus. Ed. W. Bell.	*Lond.* 8°. U.
648.	Il Penseroso. Ed. O. Elton.	*Oxford.* 8°. U.
649.	Comus. Ill. W. Blake. Ed. W. Griggs.	*Lond.* 4°. U.
	Lent by the University Library.	
650.	Garnett (R.). Life of Milton.	*Lond.* 8°. U.

1891

651.	S. A. Ed. A. W. Verity.	*Cambridge.* 8°. U.
652.	Ode, L'Allegro, etc. Ed. A. W. Verity.	*Camb.* 8°. U.
653.	Arcades and Comus. Ed. A. W. Verity.	*Camb.* 8°. U.

1892

654.	P. W. Ed. J. Bradshaw. 2 vols.	8°. UJ.
655.	P. L. Books V and VI. Ed. A. W. Verity.	*Camb.* 8°. U.
656.	" Books XI, XII. Ed. A. W. Verity.	*Camb.* 8°. U.
657.	" Books V, VIII. Ed. C. M. Lumby.	*Camb.* 8°. U.
658.	S. A. Ed. A. J. Wyatt.	*Lond.* 8°. UC.
659.	Johnson (S.). Milton. Ed. K. Deighton.	*Lond.* 8°. U.
660.	British Museum Catalogue. (Milton.)	*Lond.* F°. UJT.

1893

661.	P. W. (Sir J. Lubbock's Series.)	*Lond.* 8°. U.
662.	P. L. Books I, II. Ed. A. W. Verity.	*Camb.* 8°. U.
663.	Lycidas. Ed. O. Elton.	*Oxford.* 8°. U.
664.	L'Allegro. Ed. O. Elton.	*Oxford.* 8°. U.
665.	Comus. Ed. O. Elton.	*Oxford.* 8°. U.
666.	Bridges (R.). Milton's Prosody.	*Oxford.* 4°. U.

1894

667.	P. L. Ill. G. Doré. Ed. R. Vaughan.	*Lond.* F°. U.
668.	English Poems. Ed. R. C. Browne. New ed. by H. Bradley.	*Oxford.* 8°. U.
669.	Masson (D.). Life. New ed. Vol. 2.	*Lond.* 8°. J.
670.	" " Index Vol.	*Lond.* 8°. UC.

1895

671.	P. L. Book I. Ed. F. Gorse.	*Lond.* 8°. U.
672.	P. L. Book III. Ed. F. Gorse.	*Lond.* 8°. U.
673.	" Books III and IV. Ed. J. Sargeaunt.	*Lond.* 8°. U.
674.	" " " Ed. R. G. Oxenham.	*Lond.* 8°. U.
675.	" Book IV. Ed. M. Macmillan.	*Lond.* 8°. U.
676.	" Books VII, VIII. Ed. A. W. Verity.	*Camb.* 8°. U.
677.	L'Allegro, etc. Ed. C. E. Brownrigg.	*Lond.* 8°. U.
678.	Sonnets. Ed. A. W. Verity.	*Camb.* 8°. U.
679.	Tractate on Education. Ed. E. E. Morris.	*Lond.* 8°. U.
680.	Milton. Prize Poem by S. C. K. S. [Kaines Smith.]	*Halifax.* 8°. U.
681.	Stanford (Sir C. V.). MS. Score of Symphony 'L'Allegro & Il Pensieroso.' Op. 56.	
	Lent by the Composer.	

1896

682.	P. L. Ill. W. Strang.	*Lond.* F°. U.
	Lent by the University Library.	
683.	P. L. Books I, II. Ed. J. Sargeaunt.	*Lond.* 8°. U.

160

684.	P. L. Books VII, VIII. Ed. A. M. Trotter.	*Lond.* 8°. U.
685.	" " IX, X. Ed. A. W. Verity.	*Camb.* 8°. U.
686.	S. A. Ed. T. Page.	*Lond.* 8°. U.
687.	Lycidas. Ed. H. Evans.	*Dublin.* 8°. U.
688.	L'Allegro, etc. Ed. H. Evans.	*Dublin.* 8°. U.
689.	Early Poems. Ed. C. Sturt.	U.
690.	Masson (D.). Life. New ed. Vol. 3.	*Lond.* 8°. J.

1897

691.	P. L. (Temple Classics.)	*Lond.* 8°. U.
692.	L'Allegro, etc. Ill. W. Hyde.	*Lond.* 4°. U.
693.	Hymn. Ill. E. J. Harding and T. H. Robinson.	*Lond.* 8°. U.
694.	S. A. Ed. E. K. Chambers.	*Lond.* 8°. U.

1898

695.	P. R., S. A., etc. Ed. W. H. D. Rouse.	U.
696.	P. R. Ed. A. J. Wyatt.	*Lond.* 8°. UC.
697.	Shorter Poems. Ed. A. J. Genge.	*New York.* 8°. U.
698.	Comus. Ed. T. Page. Ed. 2.	*Lond.* 8°. U.
699.	Comus and Lycidas. Ed. A. W. Verity.	*Camb.* 8°. U.
700.	Areopagitica. Ed. J. W. Hales. New ed.	*Oxford.* 8°. U.

1899

701.	P. L. Ill. G. Doré.	*Lond.* F°. U.
702.	" Books I, II. Ed. A. W. Verity. Ed. 4.	*Camb.* 8°. U.
703.	Minor Poems. Facsimile.	*Camb.* F°. UCGK.
704.	Corson (H.). Introduction to Milton.	*New York.* 8°. U.
705.	Trent (W. P.). John Milton.	*New York.* 8°. U.
706.	Three Elegies.	*Ashendene Press, Lond.* 8°.
	Lent by S. C. Cockerell, Esq.	

1900

707.	P. W. Ed. H. C. Beeching.	*Lond.* 8°. UT.
708.	" " "	*Lond.* 12°. U.
709.	P. L. Books I-IV. Ed. J. L. Robertson.	*Edinb.* 8°. U.

| 710. | Raleigh (W. A.). Life. | *Lond.* 8°. UC. |
| 711. | Areopagitica, etc. (Temple Classics.) | *Lond.* 8°. U. |

1901

712.	Poems.	*Lond.* 8°. U.
713.	P. L. Book III. Cusack's edition. Ed. W. R. Lever.	*Lond.* 8°. U.
714.	" Evans' edition. Ed. E. H. Moreton and A. Howes.	
		Redditch. 8°. U.
715.	" " Ed. A. L. Cann.	*Bolton.* 8°. U.
716.	Comus. Ill. R. Savage. (Essex House Press.)	*Lond.* 1901. 8°. U.

Lent by the University Library.

1902

| 717. | P. L. (Doves Press.) | *Hammersmith.* 4°. U. |

Lent by T. J. Cobden-Sanderson, Esq.

718.	S. A. Ed. E. H. Blakeney.	*Edinb.* 8°. U.
719.	Lycidas. Ed. H. B. Cotterill.	*Lond.* 8°. U.
720.	Hymn on the morning of Christ's Nativity (De La More Booklets).	
		Lond. 8°. U.

1903

721.	P. W. Ed. W. A. Wright.	*Camb.* 8°. UCT.
722.	P. L. Books V, VI. Ed. Flora Mason.	*Lond.* 8°. U.
723.	Minor English Poems. Ed. H. C. Beeching.	U.
724.	Lycidas. (De La More Press.)	*Lond.* 8°. U.
725.	Byse (F.). Milton on the Continent.	*Lond.* 8°. U.
726.	Mead (L. A.). Milton's England.	*Lond.* 8°. U.

1904

727.	P. W. Ed. H. C. Beeching.	8°. U.
728.	" Ed. W. Hyde.	*Astolat Press, Lond.* F°. U.
729.	P. L. Ill. G. Doré.	*Lond.* F°. U.
730.	P. L. Book VI. Ed. H. B. Cotterill.	*Lond.* 8°. U.
731.	" " Ed. A. E. Roberts.	*Lond.* 8°. U.
732.	P. L. Book VI. Ed. A. L. Cann.	*Lond.* 8°. U.

733.	S. A. Ed. A. J. Grieve.	*Lond.* 8°. U.
734.	Minor Poems. Ed. M. A. Jordan.	*New York.* 8°. U.
735.	Comus. Ed. E. A. Phillips.	*Lond.* 8°. U.
736.	" Ed. C. J. Onions.	*Lond.* 8°. U.
737.	L'Allegro, etc. Ed. C. L. Thomson.	*Lond.* 8°. U.
738.	Areopagitica. (Eragny Press.)	*Lond.* F°. U.
739.	" Ed. H. B. Cotterill.	*Lond.* 8°. U.
740.	" Ed. C. W. Crook.	*Lond.* 8°. U.
741.	Lawes (H.). Music to Comus. Ed. C. W. Smith. (Mermaid Society.)	*Lond.* 8°.

1905

742.	Poems. Ed. W. A. Raleigh.	*Lond.* 8°. U.
743.	P. L. Ill. W. Strang.	*Lond.* F°. U.
744.	P. L. Book I. Ed. D. Salmon and W. Elliott.	*Lond.* 8°. U.
745.	P. L. Books II-V. Ed. D. Salmon and W. Elliott.	*Lond.* 8°. U.
746.	P. L. Book V. Ed. A. E. Roberts.	*Lond.* 8°. U.
747.	P. R. and S. A. (Doves Press.)	*Hammersmith.* 4°. U.
748.	S. A. Ed. C. J. Onions.	*Lond.* 8°. U.
749.	Lycidas and Sonnets. Ed. N. L. Frazer.	*Lond.* 8°. U.
750.	Prose Works. Vol. I.	*Lond.* 8°. U.
751.	Towndron (R. T.). Day Book of Milton.	*Lond.* 8°. U.
752.	Jenks (T.). In the Days of Milton.	*New York.* 8°. U.
753.	Williamson (G. C.). Milton. (Miniature Series.)	*Lond.* 8°. U.

1906

754.	P. L. Ill. W. Blake.	*Liverpool.* 4°. U.
	Lent by the University Library.	
755.	Comus, L'Allegro, etc. Ed. D. Salmon and W. Elliott.	*Lond.* 8°. U.
756.	P. L. Drama adapted by W. Stephens.	*Lond.* 8°. UT.
757.	P. L. Books I, II. Ed. A. L. Cann.	*Lond.* 8°. U.
758.	" " Ed. A. F. Watt.	*Lond.* 8°. U.
759.	Comus and other Poems.	*Camb.* 8°. U.
	Lent by the University Press.	
760.	Comus. Ill. Jessie M. King.	*Lond.* 8°. U.

1907

761. Early Poems. Ed. S. E. Goggin and A. F. Watt.   *Lond.* 8°. U.
762. Il Penseroso, etc. (De La More Press.)   *Lond.* 8°. U.
763. Areopagitica. (Doves Press.)   *Hammersmith.* 4°. K.
764. Areopagitica, etc. Ed. A. F. Watt and S. E. Goggin.

    Lond. 8°. U.
765. Lockwood (L. E.) Lexicon.   *New York.* 4°. UC.
766. Woodhall (M.). The Epic of P. L.   *New York.* 8°. U.

1908

767. Rothenstein (A.). Original Design for the forthcoming performance of Comus.

    Lent by the Artist.
768. For the original copperplates exhibited on the screen see page 132.